Rolling Stock   Cars   Buses   Trucks

Scania Cavalcade

1891–1991

Streiffert

SCANIA CAVALCADE has been published in cooperation with
Saab-Scania AB
Scania Division
S-151 87 Södertälje
Sweden
by Streiffert & Co. Bokförlag HB
Box 5098, S-102 42 Stockholm, Sweden.

© Saab-Scania AB,
Scania Division, Södertälje 1990.

Concept, editing and production Streiffert & Co. in consultation with Scania.

Chief editors Kaj Sandell and Bo Streiffert.

Text Jan-Olof Blomfeldt, Bo Björkman, Erling Matz, Per-Erik Nordström, Tiit Tamme, Kaj Sandell, Bo Streiffert and Lennart Welander.

Photographs Hans Hammarskjöld, with the exception of those on pp. 7 (top), 57, 112 (top right) (Bo Malmgren); 35, 43–45, 110–111, 112 (top left), 117, 124–125, 128–129, 134–137 (Svante Fischerström); 139 (Birger Nordin); and 3 (bottom), 4–7, 10 (bottom), 12 (top), 17 (top), 27 (bottom), 33, 40, 49 (bottom), 56 (top), 67, 92–93, 98–99, 101, 107–109, 118, 123, 133, 138 (from Scania photographic archives).

Artwork Hans Julér (pp. 140–141) and Urban Frank (pp. 142–143). Other drawings from Scania archives.

ISBN 91-7886-056-3

Photographic research Gunilla Widengren and Anita Bohlin.

Historical research 'Palle' Björkman, Willy and Ann Ekström, Lars Eriksson, Sture Gottvall, Björn Göthberg, Carl Hermelin, Kurt Isgren, Björn-Eric Lindh, John Lionell, Nils Nyström, Albert Olhager and Rolf Wedell.

Typesetting Bokstaven AB, Gothenburg.

Reproduction, printing and binding Mohndruck Graphische Betriebe GmbH, Gütersloh, Germany, 1990.

English translation Tom Byrne, Techtrans Ireland, Cork.

Editing (English edition) Johnston Editions, Gothenburg.

Contents

SCANIA CELEBRATES ITS CENTENARY in 1991. Few of the world's automakers can look back on such a lengthy, uninterrupted period of activity, coinciding as it does with almost the entire history of the automobile.

Despite two mergers, a liquidation and two changes of name, the modern Scania is the direct descendant of the company—Vagnfabriks Aktiebolaget i Södertelge—founded in 1891.

Today, Scania is the fourth largest maker of heavy trucks in the world, and is also a major producer of buses, industrial engines and marine engines. A highly export-oriented company, more than 90% of Scania's production is sold abroad, while more than half of its assembly operations are located outside Sweden.

In Sweden itself, production operations are now concentrated in several locations. As it has been since the company's foundation, the town of Södertälje remains the heart of Scania. The site on which activities commenced in those early days is now the location of the company's headquarters, which houses the central administration and marketing management functions, and is also the centre of product-development activities. One-third of all chassis are assembled in Södertälje, while bus manufacture was transferred to Katrineholm in 1967.

This long, unbroken tradition has left a clear imprint on Scania, manifested in the form of a tangible awareness of the technical and cultural importance of the company's 100-year history. In the 1950s, Scania began to buy back and restore veteran cars and epoch-making vehicles produced by the company in earlier years. In 1983, an area of the

Introduction

A carriage wheel from the 1870s preserved at Surahammars Bruk.

Major Peter Petersson, Works Manager of Surahammars Bruk, 1883–1908.

Södertälje complex was inaugurated as a museum to house the growing collection for public exhibition.

Today, the collection consists of about sixty vehicles, representing every decade of the company's history and every type of vehicle built during its existence. This even includes two railway carriages from the turn of the century, displayed in a tiny, but faithfully reproduced railway station built as part of a major expansion project completed in 1990.

Many of these often unique museum exhibits—all in working condition—are presented in this cavalcade.

Vagnfabriks-Aktiebolaget i Södertelge, 1891–1910

The fact that two railway carriages are included in the Scania Museum collection is fully appropriate, since Vagnfabriks-Aktiebolaget i Södertelge started life as a maker, not of cars, but of rolling stock.

The demand for rolling stock became enormous as the Swedish railway system expanded dramatically in the 1880s. Surahammars Bruk—an ironworks with traditions dating from the sixteenth century—was the country's largest manufacturer of wheels and other components for this market.

Shortly after Major Peter Petersson, the works manager, had suggested to his superiors that the company should undertake the production of finished carriages to capture a larger share of the market, an engineer named Philip Wersén approached the company with a proposal to establish a joint enterprise for this very purpose.

The location proposed by Wersén was the little town of Södertälje, 40 kilometres south

Vagnfabriken, circa 1895.

of Stockholm. Södertelge—as the name was then spelt—was ideally situated in relation to the expanding rail network. Furthermore, Wersén's marriage into the most prominent industrial family in the area had given him excellent contacts with the town's administrators while, as ex-production manager of the Wallenberg-owned Atlas rolling-stock works, he had also wide experience in the field.

Philip Wersén, originator of Vagnfabriken, and its head from 1891 to 1896.

This combination of factors persuaded the company to accept the proposal, with one important proviso; Wersén himself was not to be a partner, but head of rolling-stock manufacture—at a particularly generous salary. The articles of association of the new company were adopted on 11 December 1891. Since Wersén had already secured a site through his connections, operations were ready to commence little more than six months later.

Vagnfabriken (as the company was known in daily parlance) quickly became highly profitable as a supplier of goods wagons, baggage cars and bogie-mounted passenger carriages, as well as rail cars, horse trams and other products, to the Swedish State Railways (SJ) and the many private operators active at the time.

However, as the result of a dispute with the Surahammars Bruk management, the successful and dynamic Wersén resigned his post after only five years (taking with him various drawings and plans of a proposed expansion project) and immediately established a rival works which quickly outstripped Vagnfabriken in size.

A few years later, the market for rolling stock became saturated as the development

Vagnfabriken badge, 1904.

of the railways neared completion. Recognising this fact, Works Manager Petersson began to cast about for alternative products, and his interest was aroused by the novel invention which had just made its first appearance on the European continent—the 'motor-car' or 'automobile'.

Petersson appointed a young engineer named Gustaf Erikson to design Vagnfabriken's first car—and what was also to be the first Swedish car with a combustion engine. Built in 1897–98, this was an experimental model; however, the foundations for commercial production of both cars and trucks was laid during the decade which followed. In 1906, the name VABIS (comprised of the initials of the somewhat unwieldy company name) was registered as a trademark.

Despite a high reputation for quality and reliability, the production of cars and engines did not prove viable. Consequently, when the once profitable rolling-stock market finally reached saturation point towards the end of the decade (made unprofitable by excessive competition and price-cutting), the management of Surahammars Bruk began to explore ways and means of shedding the activity.

Maskinfabriksaktiebolaget Scania i Malmö, 1900–1910

In 1896, the English bicycle manufacturer, Humber & Co., established a Swedish subsidiary, known as Svenska Aktiebolaget Humber & Co., in Malmö. Four years later, the operation was taken over by a newly founded Swedish company, Maskinfabriksaktiebolaget Scania i Malmö, the articles of association being adopted on 26 January

Maskinfabriksaktiebolaget Scania in Malmö. Scania's first 1901 prototype is pictured in front of the gate.

1901. The new company expanded its activities to include the manufacture of rubber-making machines, stationary vacuum cleaners, gears and, before long, cars.

Unlike Vagnfabriken's costly philosophy of concentrating on new car and engine designs, Scania initially copied foreign designs and assembled its products from bought-in components. In 1901–02, two or three cars and a truck were built on a trial basis, followed a year later by the first series of cars (five in number) to be built in Sweden. From about 1905 on, the company was building its own engines, and the production of cars and trucks was growing.

Although Scania achieved considerable success in the marketplace, it lacked sufficient resources to expand its operations to keep pace with demand. As a result, the company's managing director, Per Nordeman, opened merger negotiations with its main competitor, Vabis, in 1910.

Per Nordeman, Managing Director of Scania from 1904 to 1911, and of Scania-Vabis until 1921.

Scania-Vabis, 1911–1921

Negotiations between Surahammars Bruk and Scania resulted in a merger between Vagnfabriken and Scania. (The manufacture of rolling stock was not included.) The agreement took effect on 18 March 1911 when AB Scania-Vabis came into existence. As the more prosperous of the two companies, Scania had a majority shareholding and Per Nordeman was appointed managing director. Situated initially in Malmö, the head office was transferred to Södertälje in 1913. Truck production was concentrated in Malmö, while Södertälje was responsible for engines, cars and light delivery trucks. At first, the new company continued to manu-

Scania radiator badge, 1902.

facture the same products as before. From the middle of the decade on, however, both the engine and vehicle ranges were renewed under the direction of August Nilsson, chief design engineer at the Södertälje factory. In the years preceding the First World War, a considerable export trade was developed with the neighbouring Scandinavian countries, Russia and the Baltic nations. Subsidiaries were established in Copenhagen and Moss (in Norway), while a repair workshop was opened in St. Petersburg.

Liquidation and reconstruction, 1921–1939

Although the company continued to expand in the domestic market during the First World War, Nordeman's ambitious efforts to transform Scania-Vabis into a major European manufacturer during the immediate postwar years were to prove disastrous. In the event, the company was forced into liquidation (under the name of Värdsholmen) as a result of the postwar depression, combined with the influx of cheap war-surplus vehicles.

However, Scania-Vabis was reconstructed and, under the leadership of Gunnar Lindmark, operations were slowly but surely re-established, transforming the company into a solid concern with a high technical reputation by the start of the Second World War. Despite this, resources remained scarce, and foreign competition compelled the company to rationalise and specialise. Car production was basically discontinued in 1925 (although a further two models were built for the company's own use as late as 1929) and the Malmö factory was closed in 1927.

Scania-Vabis, circa 1920.

Between the wars, the emphasis was shifted from truck to bus production, an activity which grew to dominate sales during the 1930s. Scania-Vabis's success in this area may be attributed partly to the development of the 'bulldog' bus, an ingenious design by August Nilsson, who was still in charge of technical development. During the 1930s, the company also won itself a high reputation for its engines. The first Scania-Vabis diesel was introduced in 1936 as the result of a cooperative agreement with the German company, Magirus. This was followed, in 1939, by the 'unitary' engine range, the first product of the component-standardisation programme which, ever since, has been a characteristic of Scania's design philosophy.

Carl-Bertel Nathorst, Managing Director of Scania-Vabis, 1940–1951, laid the foundations of today's Scania.

The Nathorst era, 1939–1951

By the end of the 1930s, the Wallenberg family (as Scania-Vabis's main shareholders) recognised the company's unexploited development potential. In 1939, Marcus Wallenberg Jr., who had then joined the Board, appointed a young rationalisation-minded graduate engineer, Carl-Bertel Nathorst, as assistant to Managing Director Gunnar Lindmark. Nathorst's succession to Lindmark's post the following year marked the start of an era which was to transform the existing company into one of the world's leading truckmakers.

Immediately on joining the company, Nathorst formulated guidelines for its future expansion. An emphasis on heavy trucks and buses, wide-ranging component standardisation, immutable quality standards and, last but not least, an export drive, were all consistent elements of his philoso-

Scania-Vabis radiator badge, 1929.

phy. Although the plans were implemented immediately, war intervened. From 1940 to 1945, Scania-Vabis became almost exclusively a defence industry, producing a comprehensive range of tanks and other armoured vehicles for the Swedish Defence Forces.

However, the expansion plans were completed, and intensive work on the development of a new postwar range of trucks and buses was undertaken as the war came to a close. By 1949, Scania-Vabis was also ready to introduce its first direct-injection diesel, a unit offering much improved performance and reliability.

Protected by the import restrictions of the postwar period and stimulated by the substantial demand for heavy vehicles to rebuild the rest of war-torn Europe, production was trebled by 1950 compared with 1939, while the proportion of exports increased to over 25%.

A major step was taken in 1948 when Scania-Vabis became Swedish general agent for Volkswagen. The addition of cars to its range enabled the company to rapidly expand and strengthen its domestic dealer network. Due in part to the highly profitable VW agency, Scania-Vabis was also in a position to finance its own major expansion programme over the next two decades.

Continued expansion and internationalisation, 1951–1968

C-B. Nathorst resigned from the post of managing director in 1951, leaving behind a company which was not only in superb shape in all departments, but was well prepared for the export drive on which it embarked with

Scania-Vabis, 1948.

the gradual lifting of import restrictions and other trade barriers in Europe. The target of 50% exports was achieved as early as 1957 and, ten years later, the volume exceeded 70%. Establishing sales subsidiaries and general agencies on an ongoing basis, the company was represented in about fifty countries on four continents by the end of the 1960s. A plant was built in Brazil in 1962, followed by an assembly plant in the Netherlands in 1965. Production was again dominated by trucks until the mid-1960s, when the output of buses increased temporarily due to the huge demand for new vehicles occasioned by the changeover to right-hand traffic in Sweden in 1967.

Intensive engine-development work continued throughout the period and Scania-Vabis consolidated its position as one of the world's leading makers of heavy diesels. Turbocharging was introduced in 1960 and what was then the most powerful diesel engine in Europe—a low-speed, turbocharged V8 developing 305 hp—was unveiled in 1969.

Leif Östling, Head of Scania Division since 1989.

Saab-Scania AB, Car Division and Scania Division, 1968–

In 1968, Scania-Vabis merged with Saab, also a Wallenberg company, and makers of military aircraft and cars, to form Saab-Scania AB. As part of the merger, the original Scania-Vabis and Saab organisations were combined to form an automotive division, and car-engine production was simultaneously transferred to Södertälje. However, profitability was not as high as expected, and a further reorganisation into Scania Divi-

sion and Car Division took place in 1972. Responsibility for the development and production of Saab petrol engines and manual gearboxes remained with Scania until 1 June 1990, when this activity was taken over by Saab Automobile AB.

Scania's position, in terms of both technical development and international market share, continued to improve throughout the 1970s and 1980s. New markets were developed continuously during the 1970s in regions such as the Middle East, and in EC countries including Italy, Germany and France, while assembly plants were opened in Australia, Iraq and several of the developing nations. In 1972, a complete truck and bus plant was established in Argentina. This facility also supplies the Brazilian plant with gearboxes in exchange for engines.

By 1990, Scania trucks and buses were in service in over one hundred markets, while about ten countries are represented by faithfully restored vehicles in the Scania Museum collection—which one observer has nicknamed 'A heaven for veteran cars'.

Scania's headquarters in Södertälje.

1891–1899

*Vagnfabriks-Aktiebolaget i Södertelge,
a subsidiary of Surahammars Bruk, was founded
in autumn 1891. Production commenced
the following year in a new 3,850-m² factory and,
by the turn of the century, 1,739 railway carriages
had been built. In 1897, however, anxious
to diversify, the company commissioned
Gustaf Erikson to develop Sweden's first
combustion-engined car. By 1899, Vagnfabriken
had 188 employees, including 18 clerical staff.*

'Gustaf Erikson's motor-car' 1897

---

*The first
Swedish-built automobile
with a combustion engine*

IN JUNE 1897, GUSTAF Erikson, Vagnfabriken's talented design engineer, pinned a new sheet of paper to his drawing board. As the man in charge of the company's new motor-car project, Erikson was about to translate into practice the experience he had gained from a recent working trip to England, France, Belgium and Germany, and the knowledge gleaned from 'The Automotor & Horseless Vehicle Journal', to which he had begun to subscribe on his return home. His work was to culminate in the design of the first Swedish-built car known to be driven by combustion engine.

Forced to abandon several of the basic principles of his very first design (which had never left the drawing board), he now threw himself eagerly into the task of designing the many new components which he realised would be necessary if the car was to be a success.

Although the engine was obviously the crucial component, Erikson believed that the problems had been resolved (at least in principle) in the original design and, following a series of improvements, a patent application for the new design was submitted in summer 1897. The patent was granted on 4 August. As before, paraffin was the chosen fuel, despite the fact that petrol was already becoming more accepted on the continent. However, since paraffin was available from every shop and was used to light almost every home in the land, people were accustomed to it. Moreover, flammable petrol was viewed

Below: Gustaf Erikson (1859–1922), 'Father of the Swedish automobile'.

with suspicion by the Swedish insurance companies.

With a design output of 6 hp, the four-cylinder engine might best be described as a hot-air unit. Since it was self-starting, it required no starter motor or crank—although the car did have to be pushed.

The engine was ready for its first bench test towards the end of 1897 (in September according to some sources). One of those present on this occasion has left us the following account:

"We ordered a better supper than usual from our landlady, to be eaten after the de-

A reconstruction of 'Gustaf Erikson's motor-car' of 1897 (also known as the 'Model A' after the designation on Erikson's original drawings). The body was of the horse-drawn carriage type, with the engine located in an enlarged compartment behind the rear seat. The reconstructed model is in the Scania Museum in Södertälje.

tions were devised and the engine was running—at least, after a fashion—by the end of the month.

On 25 August 1897, Erikson signed his name to the drawing of the actual body. Built by C.A. Carlson & Sons of Stockholm, the construction was finished in mid-September. At Surahammar, it was mounted on an iron sub-frame equipped with spoked wheels, which had been designed by Vagnfabriken in Södertälje but fitted with spokes by Carlsons.

A mere six days later, Erikson had finished the drawings of the steering column and control, throttle control and camshaft governor. While work might appear to have been advancing quite quickly, the management was becoming more and more impatient as it awaited a rapid return on its investment in the new invention. In a letter to Works Manager Peter Petersson, Erikson attempted to alleviate the Board's anxiety by submitting what might nowadays be described as an 'optimistic estimate', reporting that the running costs per 10 km of the four-seater car on which he was working would amount to 11.5 öre—7.5 öre for paraffin, 1 öre for lubricating oil and 3 öre for repairs—compared with a figure of about 15–20 öre for foreign makes.

Furthermore, Erikson estimated that the car could probably be sold for a price as low as 3,000 crowns, whereas a foreign make would almost certainly cost twice the price.

If the factory were to produce twelve cars annually, the profit—after deductions for manufacturing and administrative overheads, as well as wear-and-tear of machinery, tools and other equipment—would amount to 12,000 crowns, according to Erikson's optimistic figures. And, if the rate of production were increased to twenty-four cars annually, the profit would rise to 30,000 crowns. These figures were undoubtedly music to the ears of the Board, given that the entire factory at Södertälje had cost 17,000 crowns!

Although the date of the first test drive is not recorded, it may have taken place in February or March 1898. Erikson must have realised immediately that the engine lacked sufficient power to start both itself and the car simultaneously since he decided (as he himself put it) "to give the engine the neces-

monstration. At 10.00 p.m., the engine actually started briefly with a dreadful noise and everybody cheered. However, it stopped almost immediately and, despite the most gentle of coaxing by Erikson, refused to entertain us further with its explosions. At one in the morning—stinking of paraffin—we were obliged to wend our respective ways homeward—without our supper."

The double-acting pistons had probably seized in the cylinders as the engine became hot; the problems of cooling, lubrication and material tolerances must have caused Erikson many a headache. Nevertheless, solu-

sary head-start" by fitting a clutch and release mechanism. Design work was undertaken without delay and the car—complete with clutch—was again ready for the road by May. As yet, it did not boast a brake; however, this was probably not regarded as an urgent necessity in a car which was difficult enough to start!

By early summer 1898, Erikson considered his motor-car sufficiently reliable to risk inviting his superiors on an official test run, reputedly from Surahammars Bruk to Ålsätra and back—a distance of approximately 20 kilometres. According to one popular story, Works Manager Petersson had, to be on the safe side, ordered a horse-drawn carriage to follow the car so that he would not have to walk home if the vehicle broke down. In the event, the car managed to complete the trip, but when Erikson suggested that the time was now opportune to undertake series production of the vehicle, the manager is said to have replied: "I don't know a hell of a lot about its good points, but it certainly produces a lot of bloody smoke".

It was, perhaps, fortunate that he knew so little about cars, since the model suffered from a number of obvious defects. Like many of its foreign contemporaries, the steering control was mounted on top of a steering and control column. At the end was a steering arm which was far too long in relation to the movement of the control, in addition to which the Ackermann linkage (whose purpose was to coordinate the paths described

by the front wheels when rounding a bend) was incorrectly designed. As a result, the car was almost impossible to steer, while the performance of the engine at low revs was inherently poor. Furthermore, there was an excessive delay before the engine responded to the throttle to increase the speed of travel. Together with the steering problems, these faults made the vehicle difficult to control and driving progress fairly capricious.

However, Erikson was a stubborn and persevering individual as well as a highly talented designer. In Autumn 1898, after numerous modifications had been made to the first car, he approached Petersson and requested permission to design a completely new model. The manager's response was curt: "Mr. Erikson, get the first car to travel under its own steam, then you can start on another."

However, the 1897 car never did travel again "under its own steam". Set aside, it was not to see the light of day again until it was scrapped in spring 1899. Nevertheless, many of its parts were salvaged for use in Erikson's subsequent 1899 and 1900/01 prototypes—a wise economy, given that components such as the differential gears alone cost as much as Erikson earned in a year! As a result, parts of 'Gustaf Erikson's motor-car' are still to be seen today in the 1900/01 car, which has been restored and is now part of the collection of the Technical Museum in Stockholm.

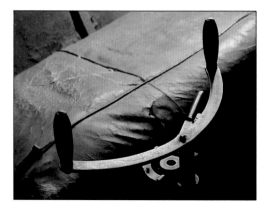

The controls of the original 'Model A' were re-used in the 1900/01 car.

Vabis bogie-type carriage

The 'Stavsjö' carriage

AROUND THE TURN OF the century, the vast forests at Kolmården were invaded by the nun moth larva. In the space of three years, 3,000 hectares of forest were destroyed, leaving the owners with the problem of disposing of more than 400,000 tree trunks.

Since the use of horse-drawn transport to move this enormous quantity of timber from almost virgin forest terrain was out of the question, the solution was to build a railway to the coast at Bråviken and to use it also for passenger traffic to and from this hitherto remote area.

With Stafsjö Järnväg in business and construction of the line under way, Vagnfabriken received an enquiry for the supply of a bogie-type passenger carriage. The company based its design on a type which had earlier been supplied to an operator in the Jönköping area, with some modification of the interior layout. The quoted price of SKr5,800 was accepted and the finished carriage was delivered on 4 June 1902.

Known as No. 2, the carriage was used until the Stavsjö line was closed in 1933, covering 6,000 to 17,000 kilometres annually during its thirty-one years of service. Disused until 1939 (when the track was taken up), No. 2 was sold that February to Eds Cellulosa AB at Edsbruk, just north of Gamleby, where the body was removed and used as a market-garden storehouse. The chassis was used as an open goods wagon on the line between the factory and the port at Helgenäs, carrying heavy pulp-bale cargoes for the next twenty-seven years. In 1966, both parts were presented to the Östra Södermanlands Railway Preservation Society in Mariefred.

Since 1967, Stavsjö No. 2 has been used during the summer season on the Society's line at Mariefred, undergoing comprehensive maintenance each winter in the Society's workshop. Although it will be eighty-nine years old in Scania's centenary year of 1991, almost all of the original parts remain, the only exceptions being the body panels (which were replaced in 1966) and the platform gates (fitted to replace the original gates which had disappeared at Edsbruk).

The Stavsjö carriage was a metal-clad, narrow-gauge, bogie-type passenger carriage divided into three compartments, two 3rd and one 2nd. Ten metres in length and 5.4 tonnes in weight, it accommodated a total of thirty seated passengers, with a further eight to ten standing on the platforms.

Right: The interior of the 2nd-class compartment.

1900—1909

Founded in the first year of the new century, Maskinfabriksaktiebolaget Scania i Malmö immediately embarked on the development of a prototype car. Its own—and Sweden's—first genuine series of production models (five in all) appeared in 1902–03. Meanwhile, development work was also continuing at Vabis and both companies built their first trucks. The Malmö factory won its first export contract—from Russia. Vabis remained primarily a manufacturer of rolling stock, producing 1,298 railway carriages and wagons, 25 self-propelled rail cars and 26 automobiles.

Scania bicycles 1900–1910

IN THE EARLY 1890s, the English bicycle makers, Humber, established a Swedish subsidiary known as Svenska Aktiebolaget Humber & Co. in Malmö. In 1900, the enterprise was taken over by a new Swedish company, Maskinfabriksaktiebolaget Scania i Malmö, the articles of association being adopted on 26 January 1901. Registered the following 16 April, the company's trademark represented the first appearance of the griffin, the mythical creature which still appears on Saab-Scania's logo today. In time, the company expanded its manufacturing operations to include rubbermaking machines, vacuum cleaners, precision gears and, before long, cars.

However, bicycles were the very first product. Although strikingly modern by present-day standards, the design was not so radically different from Leonardo da Vinci's famous 16th-century sketch.

Several models were available with a choice of nickel-plated or wooden wheels, and mudguards of steel or wood. The options even included a freewheel hub, although this added a further SKr20 to the already high price of about SKr250 – at a time when a tradesman's daily rate was three crowns!

Scania exhibited a motorcycle at the first Scandinavian motor show in Copenhagen in 1902, becoming the first Swedish company to market a factory-built motor-driven bicycle. However, production of the model was discontinued the very next year.

Made in France, the power unit was a Clement or Aster single-cylinder petrol engine delivering 1.5 hp and a top speed of about 30 km/h. The price was SKr700.

Scania bicycles were renowned for their quality. However, they were also relatively expensive and were eventually priced out of existence by cheaper, imported makes. The models pictured above were built in 1902 and are now in the Scania Museum.

The Scania motorcycle pictured here was built in 1903. The model is also preserved in the Scania Museum.

AUTOMOBILE DEVELOPMENT COMMENCED IMMEDIATELY following the establishment of Maskinfabriksaktiebolaget Scania in 1900, when forty-four year-old Hilding Hessler, managing director of the new company, assigned Works Manager Anton Svensson and the young engineer, Reinhold Thorssin, to design a car suitable for Swedish conditions. Unlike its competitor, Vagnfabriken, the company elected to base the model on foreign designs and, initially, to buy in or manufacture some of the essential components under licence.

Scania built three prototypes in 1901 and 1902. Experts have long argued as to the order in which these were produced, while it is also claimed that the third model was actually only a development of the second, usually known as the 'Thorssin' car and hitherto regarded as the first in order.

However, Scania's newly discovered drawing archives provide the answer. The first drawing, numbered A1, actually shows the only one of the prototypes which has survived for posterity. Originally painted light yellow, it was affectionately nicknamed the 'Yellow Peril'.

The car was equipped with a single-cylinder, water-cooled, four-stroke engine, probably a French Aster unit. The body was reputedly built by G. A. Jönssons Vagnfabriks

Scania 1901

The 'Yellow Peril'

Scania's second experimental car of 1901 (the 'Thorssin' car) had an air-cooled engine. Reinhold Thorssin is pictured beside driver Emil Salmson.

SPECIFICATIONS

Engine	Single-cylinder, water-cooled, four-stroke carburettor unit
Output	6 hp
No. built	1

AB in Malmö, while the lights and upholstery were supplied by the firm of Sally Mayjer of Copenhagen.

In 1923, the car was donated by Scania-Vabis to the Technical Museum in Stockholm, where it is still on view to this day.

In September 1902, the third prototype—version No. 2 of the Thorssin car, now with a water-cooled engine—probably became the first Scania car to be delivered to a customer, one Mr. J. Dankwardt of Malmö.

Scania's first model was originally light yellow and was finished in blue upholstery with gold stars. As exhibited in the Stockholm Technical Museum, however, the model is finished with a dark, crackled varnish over a top coat of indeterminate colour.

Scania 1902
Vabis 1902

—

The first trucks

IT IS NOT AN easy matter to identify the very first trucks built by the two companies which merged to form Scania-Vabis. Scania's production, in particular, is poorly documented, since most of the company's records were dispersed or destroyed when production was discontinued in Malmö and operations concentrated in Södertälje in the 1920s. All of this historically valuable documentation is believed to have literally gone up in smoke. Fortunately, however, the company's drawing archives, containing thousands of drawings, have recently been unearthed.

The records relating to Vagnfabriken's first venture into the field in which its modern successor now specialises are more complete. In this case, material including delivery journals, quotations and correspondence has been preserved together with many of the earliest drawings.

Sadly, neither of the first trucks has survived, although this is hardly remarkable in view of the small number of vehicles built in the early years (probably not more than six trucks by 1906).

Scania started to build cars at an early stage, the first series of drawings (designated A) being dated 1 July 1901, although there is no evidence to suggest that the company was also proposing to manufacture trucks at this time. Nor can this be deduced from the second series (Ab), commencing with Ab1 on 28 September 1901 and concluding with

Vagnfabriken's first truck did not survive for posterity. According to the catalogue of the 1903 Stockholm Motor Show, the 1.5-tonner had a top speed of 12 km/h. This performance may be compared with the ability of the horse to pull a 1-tonne load at 5–6 km/h.

Ab43 in early summer 1902. However, the third series (Ac), which commences on 9 January 1902, indicates that a 12-hp truck was under consideration. Unfortunately, these drawings are incomplete (lacking details of the engine and front end among other items), although a drawing of the radiator has survived.

Intensive design work on the truck was obviously in progress in early 1902, while mate-

rial dated the following September provides evidence of a further burst of activity. No subsequent drawings or other documentation relating to the first truck built by Scania in Malmö have come to light. The vehicle was driven only within the confines of the factory and was eventually scrapped. However, all indications are that it was a 1.5-tonner powered by a two-cylinder, 12-hp engine.

Unfortunately, the recently discovered drawings of the first Scania truck do not show details of the actual superstructure. Neither is this photograph of the 'complete' vehicle completely authentic. The negative has been cut at the front and touched up by an unknown hand to show the radiator.

Who, then, was its 'designer'? (Far from being an original design, the truck was probably a modified version of a French model.) At the time, Scania had two outstanding engineers in its employ, Works Manager Anton Svensson and Reinhold Thorssin, in addition to a German-born foreman named Krause, of whom little is known.

What is known is that Svensson and Thorssin were completely at odds over several technical problems, including the location of the engine. Whereas Svensson wanted it in front, Thorssin favoured a location further to the rear. In the event, Anton Svensson's proposal was approved by the managing director and it was decided, apparently during the latter half of 1902, that Scania vehicles would be equipped with front-mounted engines. By that time, Thorssin had already left Scania to join AMG (Aktiebolaget Motorfabriken i Göteborg). Interestingly enough, the only surviving picture of the truck shows that the engine was not actually at the very front, but under the driver's seat, suggesting that it was Thorssin who left his mark on the company's first venture into the heavy-vehicle sector.

Meanwhile, intensive development work was under way at Södertälje. Since Vagnfabriken was completely dependent on its production of rolling stock, it was natural that it should explore the feasibility of using Erikson's engines to drive rail vehicles. As a result, the first motor-driven rail car was tested on 8 August 1902 and was retained for further development work.

Among the engines built by Erikson was one assigned the designation E—a 9-hp, two-cylinder, opposed-piston unit with a swept volume of 2.7 litres. It was now proposed to test this engine in both a car and a truck. The indications are that the engine and truck were both built during the summer of 1902 at about the same time as the rail car was being readied for testing. By September, construction of the 1.5-tonner had advanced to the stage that only the lights remained to be fitted. At this point, it was also decided that the vehicle would be tested by the delivery firm of AB Stockholms Expressbyrå. However, this proposal fell through when the clutch failed to operate properly, and the company was obliged to carry out the test programme itself.

For obvious reasons, little was known about running costs at this time. To investigate this aspect, Vagnfabriken now undertook a series of tests (both with the truck laden and unladen) on stone-paved streets and rough country roads.

The results must have given the management little encouragement; the consumption of the fully-loaded vehicle on the streets was 50 litre/100 km, rising to 80–90 litre/100 km on the roads! The corresponding figures for

Vagnfabriken's delivery journals record that only two trucks were built between 1902 and 1906, followed by two more in 1907, three in 1908 and five in 1909. The oldest surviving model, the Vabis 1909 (see page 26), is one of the latter group. Information regarding Scania's production is more uncertain since no pre-1908 records have survived.

the unladen truck were 30 and 50 litre/100 km respectively.

At the 1903 Stockholm Motor Show, the truck was advertised for sale at SKr8,000 while, in later advertisements, it was offered at SKr7,500 without attracting any purchasers. Towards the end of the year, the vehicle was finally tested by AB Stockholms Expressbyrå, which hired it during the months of November and December. Unfortunately, the company appears to have been somewhat dubious about the novel invention and, by the following January, the truck was back in Södertälje where, as development work continued to progress rapidly, it was successively modernised.

Not until late summer 1906 did a buyer appear, although the sale was conditional on a number of modifications, among them the provision of a flat radiator and a redesigned bonnet, which altered the distinctive appearance of the front. Major modifications also resulted from the decision to fit wheels with solid rubber tyres, including the fitting of redesigned brakes—an essential improvement now that the top speed had reached a staggering 15 km/h!

Because of the time taken to complete this work, the first truck built by Vagnfabriken was not actually the first to be sold, the single model produced in 1903/04 (a 2.5-tonner finished on 15 July 1904) being purchased about a month before the 1902. For reasons unknown, the latter remained unsold until 5 May 1906 when it was delivered to St. Eriks Brewery in Stockholm as the company's first customer.

YEAR	VAGNFABRIKEN	SCANIA
1902	One 1.5-tonner	One 1.5-tonner
1903		
1904	One 2.5-tonner*	
1905		
1906		
1907	Two 3-tonners	Two or more trucks
1908	Four 3-tonners, one 1-tonner	Nine trucks
1909	Scale of truck production increases	Scale of truck production increases

*) Commenced in 1903

Vabis 1903

The first working car built by Vagnfabriken

VAGNFABRIKS-AKTIEBOLAGET I SÖDER-TELGE was a subsidiary of centuries-old Surahammars Bruk (the ironworks at Surahammar). Since it was also at Surahammar that Gustaf Erikson conducted his experimental work on the first Vabis cars (see page 10), it is natural that the collection in the Surahammars Bruks Museum should include one of Vagnfabriken's earliest products—a car with a tonneau body built in 1903. Although designed and built in Södertälje, the model is usually known as the 'Surahammar' car because of its use as a transport vehicle there in the early days—so much so that it was purchased by the ironworks in August 1909. The car appears to have continued in service until 1913, when it was replaced by a new Scania-Vabis vehicle. The retired 1903 was later found in Spännarhyttan and was meticulously restored.

The car was intended for exhibition in Stockholm in 1903 but was not completed in time. Following its first test drive that summer, it was exhibited instead at the Exposition Internationale de l'Automobile, du Cycle et de Sport in Paris, due perhaps to the fact that the body had been built by the French company, Labourdette. In fact, the car is described in a contemporary report as the 'Labourdette tonneau car'.

The model had an eventful history. Entered in the inaugural Swedish rally in 1904, its participation ended abruptly with an unscheduled takeoff from Flottsund bridge. With Gustaf Erikson at the wheel, the car was involved in yet another accident later that year when it skidded off the Södertälje-Mariefred road. Although the car was undamaged, Mrs. Erikson sustained a broken arm and several broken ribs.

The 'Surahammar' car boasts the same body, engine, transmission, spoked wheels and controls as when it left the factory at the beginning of the century, as well as another feature which was rare in those days – propeller-shaft drive.

SPECIFICATIONS	
Engine	Type E2, 2-cylinder carburettor unit
Output	10 hp
Swept volume	2.71 litre
Body	Five-seater tonneau by Labourdette
Max. speed	Approx. 15 km/h
No. built	1

Scania Type A 1903

*Sweden's oldest surviving
series-production car*

PRODUCTION OF AN INITIAL series of five cars (Scania Type A) was commenced towards the end of 1902, using the experience gained from the three prototypes built earlier that year and in 1901 (see page 17). One of the production models was exhibited at the Stockholm Motor Show in 1903, together with a Type A variant with a redesigned bonnet. The latter created a sensation by making the journey from Malmö to Stockholm in just 32 hours on the road over a period of three days. At the show, it was test driven by no less a personage than Crown Prince Gustaf, who subsequently ordered a larger version with a more powerful engine.

The royal car was delivered in January 1904—a month which was tinged with sorrow as well as joy due to the untimely death of Hilding Hessler, not yet fifty. Despite this, Hessler had made a significant contribution to the birth of the Swedish motor industry.

Car number 4 of the first series is still in existence. The model is on view at the Scania Museum in Södertälje, on permanent loan from the Technical Museum in Stockholm.

The car was delivered on board the steamer 'Södra Sverige' to Otto Bjurling of Nordstjernans Droghandel, a pharmaceutical supplies company in Stockholm. Henning Hillgren, the engineer who negotiated the sale, presented the new owner with an invoice for exactly SKr5,230:50 made up of the following items:

Weighing approximately 910 kg, the 1903 Scania Type A was 2.85 m long and 1.35 m wide. Equipped with a tonneau body, the model was a four-seater. Built by Kämper in Berlin, the 1.89-litre, two-cylinder engine developed 8 hp at 800 r/min.

Now part of the Scania Museum collection, the car is pictured here at Surahammars Bruk.

Scania Type A 1903
(continued)

8-hp motor car	5,000:00
1 spare tyre	85:00
1 spare tube	25:00
4 rim bands	100:00
4 dry batteries	20:00
Harbour dues	0:50

Payment was received on 28 September 1903.

Mr. Bjurling used his vehicle to transport both passengers and goods. In effect, he had bought a combi! The rear seat could be removed and replaced by a small goods platform, making the model ideal for his business of manufacturing, importing and exporting pharmaceutical products. His contentment with his purchase was clearly expressed in a letter addressed to the Malmö works in November 1903: "In reply to your esteemed letter of the 18th instant, I have the honour to inform you that the 8-hp tonneau automobile supplied by you in August has performed to my complete satisfaction. The vehicle has been in constant use and I have used it frequently to convey four to five persons up the steepest of hills and over the poorest of roads. Since it has, to date, rendered excellent service without any attention whatsoever, it gives me the greatest of pleasure to recommend it most highly, particularly as it is a Swedish product."

Otto Bjurling continued to drive his Scania until 7 October 1925, when he presented it to the Technical Museum in Stockholm. The car was subsequently given on

The original drawing of the two-cylinder Scania car, the Type A(d).

SPECIFICATIONS

Chassis	Type A(d)
Engine	Two-cylinder carburettor unit
Output	8 hp
Swept volume	1.89 litre
Body	Tonneau type or goods chest
Max. speed	Approx. 35 km/h
No. built	5

The Scania Type A could be equipped with a practical goods chest, which was easy to fit when required.

permanent loan to Scania in Södertälje, where it was faithfully restored.

Technical description

Originally, the ignition system consisted of a storage battery and an advance/retard mechanism. After buying the car, Otto Bjurling had this replaced by the Bosch ignition system which had been available as an option from the outset. The cooling system was of the forced circulation type with a pump and radiator, and a capacity of approximately 20 litres. The carburettor was an original Longuemare unit. The clutch was of the cone type with a friction lining, while the sophisticated lubrication system consisted of a 'lubricator'—an elegantly-shaped brass container fitted with a gauge glass and mounted on the bulkhead behind the steering wheel—from which the driver occasionally supplied the main bearings with oil by operating a hand pump. (Other points were lubricated automatically by means of an adjustable drip-feed system mounted on the lubricator.) The rear section of the gearbox (which provided three forward speeds plus reverse) incorporated a differential which drove each of the rear wheels through a half-shaft and chain-drive arrangement. The suspension consisted of semi-elliptic leaf springs all round, while the steering wheel controlled the front wheels through a gear train. Since the wheels were large, the lock was relatively small.

The brakes consisted of two independent systems, the footbrake (consisting of a drum and external band) acting on the gearbox input shaft, while the handbrake acted on the rear wheels. ('Pulling' the handbrake was unusual in that the lever was actually pushed forward!)

Vabis 1904 flatbed

Twin-axle open flatbed for bulk loads

THE MOST IMPORTANT ASPECT of railway development in Sweden was the fact that, for the first time, large quantities of goods could be transported over long distances.

Freight traffic also became decisive to the economic prosperity of the operators, bulk loads such as ore, coal and timber being the principal—and most lucrative—cargoes. In the south, many lines survived almost exclusively on the transport of sugar beet.

At a time when alternative means of personal transport were few, passengers were obliged to take second place to freight, travelling on 'mixed' trains which stopped at every station for the purpose of shunting goods wagons. At the turn of the century, therefore, a journey such as the 120 kilometres from Stockholm to Eskilstuna took about four and a half hours to complete.

Goods wagons designed specifically for the above-mentioned cargoes were soon developed, one being a twin-axle open flatbed with low, hinged sideboards for commodities such as coal. This type was also equipped with removable side posts to hold the huge stacks of timber which comprised one of the commonest cargoes carried on many Swedish railways.

Designated N 1, large numbers of the wagon and its variants were built for the Swedish State Railways (SJ) and private operators alike, narrow-gauge versions included. By 1907, SJ had over 5,000, equivalent to about one-fifth of its entire goods fleet.

In all, Vagnfabriken produced 600 Type N 1 wagons, including 160 for SJ. Fortunately, one standard-gauge version has survived and has been restored, as far as possible, to its former condition. Now part of the Scania Museum collection, the 7.7-metre wagon had a wheelbase of 3.75 m and a capacity of 12 tonnes.

Vabis 1909

---

*The oldest
surviving Vabis
truck*

NOW ON VIEW IN the Scania Museum in Södertälje, this resplendent old model is the oldest Vabis truck in existence. The vehicle was built in 1909 and delivered the same year to AB Reinhold Bergmark, shoe manufacturers, of Gothenburg at a price of SKr10,500.

Bearing the registration O84, the truck was equipped with a V2 engine developing 15–18 hp. However, prior to its re-registration in 1916 (when it became O35), this had been replaced by the more powerful F4, a four-cylinder, side-valve petrol engine with

an output of up to 24 hp. In 1918, the truck was bought by Janne Alarik Claesson, a fish merchant, also of Gothenburg.

In 1923, the truck was again sold, this time to Oskar Hultén of Åmål. At this stage, it must have been in the 'well-used' category, since Hultén paid only 500 crowns for his new purchase.

In the course of a visit to Scania in 1976, when he renewed acquaintance with the old family treasure, Oskar's son, Holger recalled some of the uses to which the truck was put:

"As a youth, I often drove from Östra Kors-

SPECIFICATIONS	
Chassis	2-tonne type
Wheelbase	3.30 m
Engine	Type E2V, 2-cylinder carburettor unit
Output	15–18 hp
Swept volume	2.71 litre
Super-structure	Rigid platform
Payload	2,000 kg
No. built	3

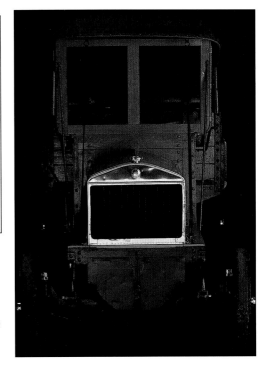

The Vabis 1909 now on view in the Scania Museum has a four-cylinder, Type F4 petrol engine under the bonnet. This replaced the original engine some time before 1916.

difficult to drive on grass and similar surfaces. As a result, it was only used at harvest time after 1928.

However, it remained on the farm, parked in a shed until 1940, when it was bought by Scania-Vabis for 800 crowns. Two years later, it was acquired by the Technical Museum in Stockholm, which subsequently presented it on permanent loan to the Scania Museum.

byn, in Åminskog, to Åmål and back. At that time, we made bricks on the farm and I delivered them to the town. The truck could carry two tonnes, which was considered a lot at the time. What we used to call roads were in atrocious condition and it took two hours, changing down to take every hill, to cover the 20 kilometres. Coming home took half an hour less, but then I had no load."

The truck was used at Korsbyn for five years before it was laid up. It could not be used in winter since the solid rubber tyres were completely smooth, while it was also

Right: In 1925, the Vabis 1909 took part in the midsummer celebrations at Östra Korsbyn. At the wheel is Oskar Hultén.

Vabis car, 1909

The oldest privately-owned Vabis car

ONLY IN LATE 1909, after many vicissitudes, did Mjölkningsmaskin AB of Stockholm finally take delivery of the Vabis car which it had ordered early in 1909. The vehicle was delivered on 15 October rather than 15 July as promised.

The purchaser was patently annoyed. At the beginning of August, the head of the company, Otto Rooth, wrote to his good friend Karl Erik Öhman, then works manager of Surahammars Bruk, the parent company of Vagnfabriken in Södertälje. The letter was short and to the point: "Had I had the faintest idea that Vagnfabriken would be so incapable of fulfilling an order, I would obviously never have given them the contract, but would have placed the business elsewhere."

In all fairness, it must be said that Vabis had more than its share of ill luck with this particular car. The coachbuilder was behind in his work – not entirely surprising at a time when a body was a complicated and fairly unusual structure – and just as the situation was beginning to look more promising at the end of the summer, the company was hit by a month-long national industrial strike which added further to the infuriating delay.

Neither could the deal have been especially profitable for Vagnfabriken, although the best was made of the situation. The company managed to extract a small penalty from the coachbuilder, and also secured a reduction in price of 20 crowns in the form of a 1% cash discount!

Mjölkningsmaskin AB, in turn, deducted SKr240 from the originally agreed price of SKr8,881.

The firm used the car only for a short period to tour the local farms in search of buyers for its milking machines. After two years, it was sold to Bröderna Johanssons Åkeri (Johansson Brothers Taxi Company) in Bollnäs, where it was used as a taxi for the next decade. Another pair of brothers, Lars and Jonas Larsson, together with a neighbour from Röstebo, outside Bollnäs, then bought the old Vabis from Johanssons and used it as a private car until 1926.

Jonas Larsson finally acquired the car himself and drove it home to Söderala some-

Originally, the Vabis 1909 was equipped with a G4, four-cylinder, carburettor engine with side valves. As part of the comprehensive overhaul carried out at the Södertälje works in 1913, this was replaced by the existing 20-hp G42.

had been converted into a childrens' playhouse!

Thus, Erik Örtlund at last acquired the authentic part which he needed to reproduce the body of the original Vabis 1909, the oldest surviving private car built by Vagnfabriks-Aktiebolaget i Södertelge.

SPECIFICATIONS	
Chassis	Type 2S
Engine	Type G4, 4-cylinder, side-valve carburettor unit
Output	12–14 hp
Swept volume	2.01 litre
Body	Limousine type with open driving seat
Max. speed	Approx. 50 km/h
No. built	3 (19)

time during the 1930s. He was almost certainly thinking of renovating it himself and it is known that he at least worked on the magneto. When Erik Örtlund of Borlänge bought the car from Jonas's son, Börje, in 1984, the dismantled parts were stored in about twenty crates alongside the stripped-down frame.

The car was 95% intact and, although somewhat dilapidated, was not expected to be unduly difficult to restore. There was, however, a complication. In 1913, the vehicle had been sent to Södertälje for a complete overhaul, including replacement of the engine. Unluckily, the Scania-Vabis factory was devastated by a major fire at exactly that time and the unique body was so badly damaged that it was simply replaced by an open phaeton body.

By the mid-1980s, the vehicles restored by Erik Örtlund included a Model A Ford, a 1924 Willys-Overland and a 1914 Wanderer motor-bike.

Now that he had a truly unique vehicle in his possession, he was anxious to carry out a thorough job. Deciding to restore the car to its original 1909 condition, he 'rejected' the 1913 body. The problem now was to locate a Swedish-built car body from the first decade of the century. Back in the 1960s, Erik had searched in vain for an old body rumoured to be located somewhere in Horndal. Twenty years later, this elusive component again began to occupy his thoughts. Determined to establish whether or not it existed, he resumed the search— and discovered why he had been unsuccessful on the first occasion.

The body (obviously Swedish-built) had originally been ordered for a Horch owned by Count von Rosen of Horndal. However, it was never used and, sometime during the 1920s,

1910–1919

*The decade witnessed a breakthrough
in vehicle production for Scania-Vabis. During
the period, the company built a total of
1,147 vehicles, including 475 of the 830 or so car
chassis produced before this activity was
discontinued. Export sales represented the most
remarkable aspect, no less than 25% of production
being sold abroad. The railway era came to an
end in 1911 after a further 135 wagons and
carriages had been manufactured, although
a further 17 self-propelled rail cars
were produced up to 1914.*

The first buses

The 'Nordmark' bus.

Remarkably enough, it is almost impossible to identify—with absolute certainty—the very first bus built in Sweden.

If a bus is defined as a conveyance designed to carry passengers on a regularly scheduled basis and equipped (as a minimum) with permanent sides, windows, a roof and door, it is more than likely that a Scania, Vagnfabriken (Vabis) or Scania-Vabis was the first. (Although it is possible that the first Tidaholms Bruk model appeared earlier, the details of its delivery are vague.)

However, all of the evidence suggests that the 'Nordmark' bus was the first Swedish-built model to enter regular service. Equipped with a chain-driven chassis built by Scania in Malmö, and an engine and body by Vabis in Södertälje, the bus was delivered by Scania-Vabis to Nordmarkens Automobiltrafik Aktiebolag on 17 October 1911.

While awaiting delivery of the vehicle, the company was given the use of a Scania-Vabis truck, the platform of which was probably fitted with some type of bench seating.

Entering scheduled service with Rothoffs Bussbolag of Landskrona on 4 June 1912, the next bus was used initially on the Landskrona-Borstahusen-Karlslund route, after which its history is somewhat hazy.

The propeller shaft-driven model was a Vabis which had probably been assembled in 1910 (prior to the merger of the two companies) but which, for some unknown reason, was not used in regular service until two years later.

Delivered in 1913, the third bus was also bought by Rothoffs. However, this was a chain-driven model fitted with the old, rounded Scania radiator.

SINCE UNIQUE EVENTS ARE often surrounded by myths and legends, it is not surprising that so many tales are told about the Scania-Vabis 1911, the vehicle which may justifiably be called Sweden's first genuine bus. These are just some:

– The seats were covered with rough moosehide to prevent the passengers from falling off with the shaking. (In actual fact, it was the roads, not the bus, which were poor.)

– The wheels created constant problems. The bus had solid rubber tyres which were continually splitting. At first, barbed wire was used in an attempt to fix the fault, then the wheels were shod with iron 'tyres'. Nevertheless, they still had to be repaired after every journey.

– Missing the bus was not a problem – anybody could catch it by running after it.

– The incredible rattling of the vehicle caused horses to bolt, making it highly unpopular with the local farmers. On one occasion, they dug a pit, and covered it with twigs and stones to catch the bus (successfully, it is said!).

– Driver Hjalmar Kroksén was a real

Scania-Vabis 1911

———

The 'Nordmark' bus

Hjalmar Kroksén, driver of the 'Nordmark' bus.

ladies' man. Jealous farmhands sometimes blocked the road to stop the bus and give him a good hiding.

However, the true history of Scania-Vabis 1911 is also full of odd facts.

The bus was ordered in 1911 by Nordmarkens Automobil Trafik Aktiebolag. A region of the Swedish province of Värmland, adjoining the Norwegian border, Nordmark is a heavily forested and remote area. Precisely why six men in this desolate place established Sweden's first bus company is only one of the mysteries surrounding the vehicle. It is certainly true that they had no experience of road traffic; in fact, it is likely that automobiles had travelled the atrocious roads in the area only twice before – once in 1902 and once in 1905! Nevertheless, the minutes of the first meeting of the new company reported in succinct tones:

"The purpose of the enterprise is to improve communications in the district of Nordmark, and to facilitate communications with the railways and other major traffic arteries."

The bus was to run between Åmot and År-

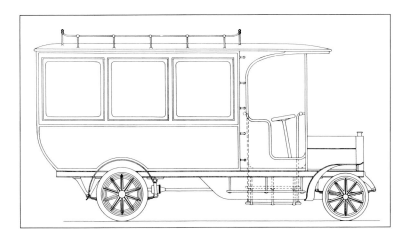

jäng. Established in November 1910, the company made immediate enquiries for a suitable vehicle and quotations were obtained from Maskinfabriks Aktiebolaget Scania i Malmö; Gjestvangs Handels & Fabriks Aktiebolag, Stockholm; Tidaholms Bruks Aktiebolag; Aktiebolaget E. Lundvik & Co., Stockholm and Anders Skog, Gothenburg.

Three months later, the men of Nordmark had made their choice – a Scania – on the

The 'Nordmark' bus was built by Scania in Malmö on a chain-driven truck chassis, and was equipped with its body and engine by Vabis in Södertälje.

This 1910 body drawing shows a Vabis propeller shaft-driven bus. The body is reminiscent of the 'Nordmark' bus.

basis of "excellent reports and satisfactory conditions", to quote the minutes of a company meeting held in February 1911. Director Nordeman of Scania was present on this occasion and a contract was signed on the spot, stipulating that a fully-covered automobile with a 30-hp engine was to be delivered on 15 May 1911 at a price of SKr12,936. Scania also became part-owner of the company, acquiring 25% of the shares.

During the next few weeks, argument appears to have raged in the Värmland forests. Would the bus be able to negotiate the dreadful roads and the steep inclines? Would it take fifteen passengers?

Scania was again contacted and the contract was modified. According to the final order (No. 2854 B), the bus was to be powered by a 34-hp engine and the price was revised to SKr14,500. Signed by Scania-Vabis (which had been established in the interim), the order listed the following specifications:

Type: 1½-tonner. Engine: 100 x 140 mm, 30–36 hp, to be manufactured in Södertälje. Frame construction: 120-mm members. Tyres: 760 x 70 mm (front) and 950 x 100

(rear). Headlamps: 2. Gas unit: 1. Paraffin lamps: 2. Rear light: 1. Odometer: 1. Snow chains: 2, for rear wheels.

It was on 17 October 1911 that the company, in the persons of Adolf Manby from Årjäng and Nils Eklund from Trollesbyn, took delivery of the bus. Following a test run from Södertälje to Stockholm, they reported that:

"The automobile performed well on a poor road, reaching an average speed of 20 kilometres per hour."

The first scheduled run over the Åmot-Årjäng route took place on 30 November, the light-coloured bus with its many windows arousing enormous interest. "The new automobile performed excellently", commented a gratified Board.

The bus also appears to have given satisfactory service that winter, although a machine from a local paper mill blocked the road for several weeks, preventing it from completing its run. The net profit in the first year of operation was 1,472 crowns and 32 öre.

However, the Nordmark roads are invariably better in winter than in summer, and it was the following summer of 1912 that the problems began – split tyres, terrified horses, ambushes set by angry farmhands, and so on.

The profit that year was a mere 98 crowns, improving slightly to 349 crowns in 1913. At this juncture, the authorities also took a hand and the bus was prohibited from operating during Årjäng market. With horses becoming too frightened and their drivers too angry, the risk of accidents was considered too high.

A trip in the first Swedish-built bus was an event worth recording. These eager passengers are pictured prior to their departure from Årjäng.

The Nordmark winter roads were kinder to the bus than the rutted summertime surfaces. The model is pictured here with snow chains on the rear wheels.

By 21 June 1914, the Board had had enough, deciding unanimously that "regular bus traffic is to cease", although the vehicle itself was to give several more years of service. Purchased by driver Hjalmar Kroksén, it was used to carry troops returning on leave, church societies on excursions and various other groups. Indeed, it might be said that Scania-Vabis 1911 was also Sweden's first tourist coach! However, the roads eventually took their toll; the headlamps shook loose, the chainguards fell off, the mudguards became dented and the ironshod wheels continued to give problems. After just a few years, Kroksén himself gave up. The body was removed and used as a children's playhouse, while the chassis, with its powerful engine, was used to haul timber from the forests and firewood to the glassworks at Glava. Sometime in the early 1920s, the chassis was driven onto the frozen Stora Gla lake, where it sank through the ice the following spring. And so, the first bus disappeared, perhaps forever. Who knows?

"But it served us well to the very end," relates Bengt Vik from Älgå. "The rear wheels were fitted with 'studs' (which were simply bolts driven through the tyres and held by nuts on the inside) and 3-inch birch skids were fitted in place of the front wheels. Like this, it could haul three fully-loaded sleds of wood – and a gang of youngsters clinging on behind..."

These were to be the last 'passengers' carried by the first Swedish bus.

IT WAS A SIGNIFICANT contract which the Royal Swedish Post Office in Stockholm awarded Scania-Vabis on 23 May 1913—an order for no less than thirteen post vans at a total cost of SKr117,075, equivalent to about SKr3.1 million today. Of the thirteen vehicles, seven were of the type illustrated above. The body was mounted on a standard chassis from the new range of vehicles introduced by Scania-Vabis shortly before.

The post office in Gothenburg having acquired vehicles of the same type the previous year, it was now the turn of Stockholm to modernise its fleet. In all, no less than twenty-five new vans of different types were ordered at a single stroke.

Since the Stockholm postal authorities had no qualified drivers, Scania-Vabis offered both to provide drivers and to carry out the necessary repair work in what was one of the first comprehensive service agreements ever concluded in Sweden.

In the 1950s, when Scania began its search for vintage vehicles suitable for renovation and display in its projected museum, one of its finds was this particular post van, which was used to deliver parcels to post offices around Stockholm from 1913 to 1927.

Scania-Vabis 1913

Royal Swedish Post Office van

However, it was not until the late 1960s that the resident mice were evicted from the cooling system, renovation work commenced and a search undertaken for the parts which had disappeared over the years. Working alongside Scania's own experts, the staff of the Post Office service workshop at Ulvsunda gave unstintingly of their spare time to create something of a vintage 'jewel'.

With the merger of Scania and Vabis, car production was transferred to Södertälje, where this attractive vehicle—a gift from the Post Office Museum in Stockholm—is now on view in the Scania Museum.

SPECIFICATIONS	
Chassis	Type 2 S
Engine	Type G 42, 4-cylinder, side-valve carburettor unit
Output	16–20 hp
Swept volume	2.27 litre
Body	Box type
Payload	400 kg
No. manufactured	7 (78)

Scania-Vabis Type I 1914

*'Olle',
a unique
family
heirloom*

SOME OF THE CARS in this volume are undoubtedly of greater technical interest than the phaeton-bodied Scania-Vabis Type I which was handed over to District Medical Officer A.G. Nyblin and his 18-year old son, Sigvard, in Södertälje on 6 November 1914. Nevertheless, this particular model is unique (in international as well as Swedish terms) in having had only three owners—all members of the same family—in its almost eighty years of existence!

Monica Hägglund, daughter of the late Sigvard Nyblin and his wife, Ebba, has given the family treasure on loan to the Scania Museum in Södertälje. The following account of the car, which was affectionately nicknamed 'Olle', is based on her recollections.

The car was collected in Södertälje by Monica's grandfather, Dr. A. Gustaf Nyblin, for use in his work as District Medical Officer in Gnesta. It was the second car to appear in the area. Dr. Nyblin was accompanied to Sö-

dertälje by his son, Sigvard, who was then eighteen years old and who had long been interested in cars. Among other activities, he had been a spectator at several of the Royal Swedish Automobile Club's rallies. Sigvard Nyblin had learned to drive at an early age in an old car (probably an English 'Star') which the family had bought second-hand in 1912.

"We have a letter from AB Scania-Vabis, dated 12 March 1912, in which they thank my grandfather for his enquiry for a small car", recalls Monica. According to an entry in her father's diary, this was in reply to a letter in which Dr. Nyblin had enquired if the company could manufacture a car for about 5,000 crowns. Later that year, the factory produced a prototype based on a chassis which bore a strong resemblance to the German 'Protos' and was fitted with a temporary body. The car was tested over rugged country roads, including a particularly steep hill which Dr. Nyblin had stipulated would have to be negotiated. Although the trial was successful and the good doctor duly placed an order for the car, delivery was delayed for some time for a variety of reasons (probably including the fire at Scania-Vabis in Södertälje in 1913).

According to an existing copy of the delivery docket (dated 30 October 1914), the car cost 7,584 crowns, including some extra equipment. Although it was to be finished in ivory with red leather uphol-stery, Sigvard's diary reports that "the car was returned to Scania-Vabis on 16 November for repainting because it was light yellow instead of ivory as ordered. It is now to be painted in a mahogany colour."

Dr. Nyblin was granted his 'certificate of competence' as a driver on 26 July 1912 and, that summer, he received permission from the authorities in Ny-köping to use the car on "roads of 3.6 metres and less in width" in the district of Daga, enabling him to make his calls in his Scania.

'Olle's' attractive dashboard is decorated with badges from many Swedish and inter-national veteran-car rallies.

Nicknamed 'Olle' by the family, the car was driven by Dr. Nyblin until his death in 1923. It then passed to Sigvard, who drove it until just a few years before his own death in 1980. 'Olle' was actually used as a utility car until well into the 1950s, when the family acquired a more 'comfortable' model. However, it continued in service (usually driven by Sigvard), taking part in many rallies as well as a series of official events. When King Gustav Adolf VI visited Scania-Vabis during the company's 75th anniversary celebrations in 1966, he was driven in it with Marcus Wallenberg and Scania President Gösta Nilsson, while the present monarch, King Carl Gustaf XVI, rode in the Type I with a friend while he was still Sweden's 'Little Prince'.

Shortage of petrol during the Second World War caused 'Olle' to be laid up in a barn belonging to a farmer at Bocksboda in Kilsbergen, where the family had a summer house. When the war was over, the car was simply filled up and restarted without any attention whatsoever. During the postwar years, it was used mainly for driving from

Örebro (where it was garaged) to Kilsbergen, where it was better able to negotiate the hilly, rutted, gravelled roads than the Mercedes which Sigvard had purchased around that time.

The car has acquitted itself honourably in a series of rallies both at home and abroad. The first of these in the thirty-five years or so in which it has been 'shared' by Scania and the Nyblin/Hägglund family was the British Silver Jubilee Rally held at Stratford-on-Avon in the mid-1950s. Vintage cars from all corners of the world were invited to this prestigious event, 'Olle' being the only Swedish entry among 207 cars from the 1898–1917 period. In the rally itself, it was one of only eight entries to finish without penalty points, taking 5th place, and was placed 21st in the overall event. And, in one respect, it was in a class of its own; it was the only entry to have been in continuous service ever since its delivery!

Monica Hägglund concludes her reminiscences: "I represent the third generation of owners—and a little member of the fifth generation has just appeared on the scene. So it looks as though this unique sequence of ownership may go on forever. We'll be celebrating a centenary too!"

SPECIFICATIONS	
Chassis	Type I (2121)
Kerb weight	1,250 kg
Engine	Type I (1241), 4-cylinder, side-valve carburettor unit
Output	22 hp
Swept volume	2.1 litre
Body	Five-seater phaeton
Max. speed	Approx. 65 km/h
No. built	123 (305)

Scania-Vabis fire-engines 1912–1919

To PURCHASE A MOTORISED fire-engine back in the Olympic year of 1912 called for a certain degree of courage. Nevertheless, this is exactly what the Stockholm city fathers did—although they hedged their bets by buying a German machine. But to order an unproven Swedish vehicle at that time might well have been called foolhardy. However, Norrköping Town Council did—and so, in 1912, Scania-Vabis delivered its very first fire-engine, the chassis of which was built in Malmö, and the engine and gearbox in Södertälje.

By early 1913, the crew had been trained in the operation of the new equipment and it was duly commissioned, rendering long and faithful service until it was scrapped in 1950.

Delivered in 1914, the second Scania-Vabis also gave long service and was retired only in 1940.

The third unit, which was delivered on 22 June 1915, is still in excellent condition. Just a few months older than its splendid Helsingborg counterpart (page 40), it is the oldest Scania-Vabis fire-engine still in existence.

Bearing the registration number E211, this elegant red vehicle was also retired from service in 1940, although it was retained as a standby unit for several years more until it was sold back to Scania-Vabis in Södertälje in 1953. In the early 1980s, the chassis and superstructure were completely and faithfully renovated over a period of several years by the staff of Norrköping Fire Brigade, while the engine and gearbox were reconditioned under the direction of the Scania Museum.

This work should, perhaps, have been carried out somewhat earlier, to judge by the minutes of a meeting held by Norrköping Town Council in 1939 to discuss the estimates for the coming year. One of the items on the agenda was the replacement of the

Scania-Vabis 1915

Norrköping Fire Brigade

fire-engine purchased in 1915. In arguing the case for replacement, it was emphasised that "on a couple of occasions, the vehicle has broken down while on duty and has had to be towed back to the station. On other occasions, its speed has been limited to no more than walking pace. What such obvious defects have led the general public to think of the municipal firefighting service need hardly be imagined."

When the engine was dismantled for com-

SPECIFICATIONS	
Chassis	Type DLa Special
Wheelbase	4.05 m
Engine	Type K-1, 4-cylinder, side-valve carburettor unit
Output	60 hp
Swept volume	8.59 litre
Equipment	24-metre ladder; 1,500 l/min pump
No. built	17 (42)

plete overhaul at Södertälje, it was obvious that it had overheated; some pistons had seized and one was cracked. Today, however, the unit is once more in 'new' condition.

Originally equipped with a rear-mounted RAG pump delivering 1,500 l/min at a pressure of 9 kg/cm^2, the vehicle was a 3-tonne combined rescue and firefighting unit.

In October 1915, the unit was equipped with a mechanical, 24-metre tilting ladder supplied by Allmänna Brandredskapsaffä-ren of Stockholm. Compared with the price

This DLa Special is the oldest Scania-Vabis fire-engine still in existence. It was delivered to Norrköping Fire Brigade on 22 June 1922.

of SKr20,000 for the vehicle and pumping plant, the cost of the ladder (SKr3,800) must have seemed excessive. However, it proved to be worth every penny. When the engine was retired in 1940, the ladder was transferred to its successor. It continued in use until 1948, when it was reunited with the original vehicle, on which it has remained to this day!

(Continued)

HELSINGBORG FIRE BRIGADE became motorised as early as 1915. The first combined rescue and firefighting unit has been preserved for posterity—in more beautiful condition than ever—thanks to the enthusiastic work of the Helsingborg Fire Service Pensioners' Association.

The vehicle rendered about thirty years of service before its retirement to the museum at Fredriksdal. It was acquired by the firemen themselves in 1969 and restored completely by the early 1970s, a labour of love which took approximately 1,200 hours.

Costing SKr26,320 originally, the present value of the vehicle can only be a matter of conjecture.

Scania-Vabis 1915

———

Helsingborg Fire Brigade

OF THE FIVE FOUR-WHEEL drive fire-engines supplied to the various Swedish services, only one is still in existence—that delivered on 19 September 1919 to Södertälje Fire Brigade, with which it remained in service for a quarter of a century. Acquired by the Stockholm Technical Museum in the 1940s, it was later presented to Scania.

Faithfully restored, it was subsequently exhibited for the approval of the man who was usually behind the wheel during its

Scania-Vabis 1919

———

Södertälje Fire Brigade

many years of service—Johan 'Fireman' Johansson.

Although of advanced design, many remember the engine for just one unique feature—the unusual siren in the form of 'organ pipes' mounted at the mouth of the exhaust pipe.

Driven by a Type 1546, four-cylinder, side-valve, petrol engine developing 50 hp, the vehicle cost SKr39,500.

Scania-Vabis 1917

"The ideal car for the gentleman driver"

"THE IDEAL CAR FOR the gentleman driver" read the slogan for the new Scania-Vabis Type I light car in advertisements published during the First World War. The power of advertising was evident even then – the first users of the new model, known today as the 'Kälarne' car, were gentlemen from the Swedish Defence Administration.

The 1916 Type I phaeton-bodied car pictured above was delivered, in September 1917, to Lieutenant-Colonel F. W. Löwenborg, District Commander in Haparanda. The price was SKr9,850. After serving as a staff car in Boden for some years, the vehicle was acquired by the Army Command in Östersund. In 1924, it passed into civilian hands and was owned, in turn, by E. Sjöström, a telegraph repairman from Östersund, and N. J. Eriksson, a Grimdalsby farmer, before ending up in Kälarne (to which it owes its nickname).

On 13 March 1958, an agreement was made between hauliers J. W. Andersson of Kälarne and Scania-Vabis that the car would be returned to Södertälje for renovation. The work was completed in 1965 and,

the following year, this now-familiar model made its first spectacular appearance on the rally scene when it was driven from Stockholm to Malmö in a semi-serious attempt to break the existing veteran-car 'record' for the trip. In this it was remarkably successful, reaching the premises of Scania-Bilar in Malmö in 19 hours and 20 minutes, despite running out of petrol a few kilometres short of its goal. It was a notable performance by a car almost fifty years old!

SPECIFICATIONS	
Chassis	Type I (2121)
Engine	Type I (1241)
Output	22 hp
Swept volume	2.1 litre
Body	Five-seater phaeton
Max. speed	Approx. 65 km/h
No. built	123 (305)

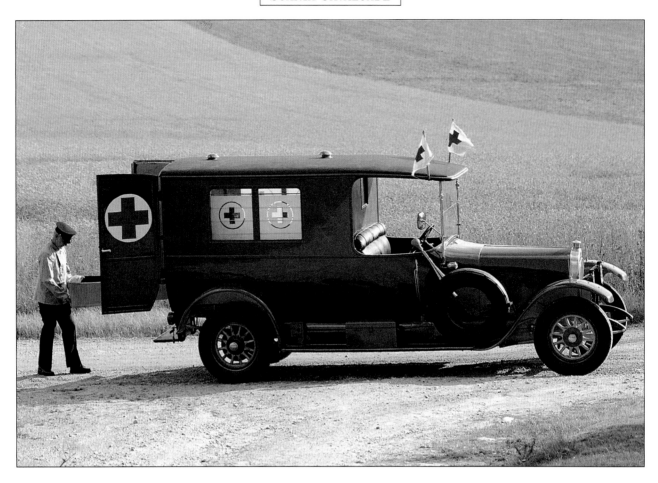

SCANIA-VABIS CAR CHASSIS were used to carry several types of superstructures which were also produced in Södertälje. As one such special application, ambulances were built in versions accommodating anything from a single stretcher to no less than eighteen! In the latter case, the vehicle was built on a tractor unit and equipped with two trailers, each carrying six patients.

The delivery records show that the City of Stockholm Health Authority received its first ambulance from Vagnfabriken as early as 27 August 1910, followed by a further twenty or so until car production was discontinued by the company. None of these has survived.

Happily, however, one elegant example of the type is still in existence. Now on display in the Scania Museum, the vehicle was delivered on 19 November 1919 to the Fredrikstad public hospital in Norway, where it remained in service until the Second World War. Although it was retired and replaced by a more modern vehicle, parts for its successor proved impossible to obtain during the

Scania-Vabis 1919

A prize-winning ambulance

war and the trusty old servant was recalled to duty until 1946, making a total service life of twenty-seven years.

Superbly restored by the Norwegian Veteran Car Club, the vehicle was sold to Scania-Vabis in 1958. In 1970, it was further refurbished prior to its entry in the famous London to Brighton Rally, in which its special charm won it the coveted prize for elegance.

SPECIFICATIONS	
Chassis	Type III (2453)
Wheelbase	3.72 m
Engine	Type III (1546), 4-cylinder, side-valve carburettor unit
Output	50 hp
Swept volume	5.03 litre
Body	Ambulance with 1 stretcher
Max. speed	Approx. 85 km/h
No. built	7 (51 Type III)

THE TRUCKS BUILT BY Scania-Vabis during the first half of the 1910s were largely based on Scania's pre-merger designs, and it was well into the decade before these were superseded by more modern types. About this time, however, the older chassis and engines were given new designations, making it difficult now to research Scania-Vabis's earliest trucks.

One truck from this transition period has been preserved in original condition, with the exception of the cab and the pneumatic tyres which have replaced the solid rubber tyres.

The model is a 2-tonne, chain-driven CLc which was delivered from the Malmö works, on 15 October 1919, to A. F. Carlsson's shoe factory in Vänersborg. It was Carlsson's first goods vehicle. The body was probably built by Emil Salonens Snickerifabrik, a joinery in the same town, where P371 (the truck's registration number) soon became a familiar sight on the streets.

Driver 'Lille-Kalle' (or 'Little Charlie') normally drove the truck locally, delivering

Scania-Vabis 1919

A veteran, chain-driven truck in almost pristine condition

SPECIFICATIONS	
Chassis	Type CLc
Wheelbase	3.65 m
Engine	Type II (1344)
Output	30 hp
Swept volume	2.82 litre
Payload	2,000 kg
No. built	126 (203)

hides to the factory's tannery or finished shoes to the harbour for onward shipment by the Göta Canal. A reminder of his diminutive stature is still to be seen in the shape of the thick wooden block which helped him reach the accelerator!

The truck was nicknamed the 'Rumbler' by the locals because of the characteristic noise made by its hard, solid-rubber tyres on the cobblestone streets of the town.

After long service, the truck was sold to landowner Lennart J:son Mark of Kalltorp Farm in Upphärad. Its drawbar indicates that it was used to pull farming implements in the fields, while its relatively low platform also made it suitable for loading grain—and, of course, manure—causing the faithful old servant to become known by the new sobriquet of 'Dung-carrier'.

The truck remained in service until 1946, when it was stored in a barn outside Vänersborg. Rediscovered in 1961, it was bought for the Scania collection.

1920–1929

As a result of the increasing financial difficulties which it encountered towards the end of the 1910s, AB Scania-Vabis went into liquidation in 1921, but was subsequently rebuilt. The Malmö factory was closed, activities concentrated in Södertälje and car production discontinued. A total of 1,714 vehicles (427 of which were buses), was manufactured during the decade. However, operations proved unprofitable and losses were sustained in six of the ten years. One vehicle per working day was being built as the end of the decade approached, by which time the workforce totalled four hundred.

Post bus 1922

Scania-Vabis post buses broke the winter isolation of remote northern Sweden

MOTORING MADE RAPID PROGRESS in Sweden during the 1920s—at least during the warm, dry months. However, it became a much more difficult proposition as winter seized the country in its icy grip. Under these conditions, the horse-drawn sled was a much more efficient means of transport, even where there were no roads.

Winter road maintenance was the subject of lively discussion at this time. For example, in the September 1923 issue of the motoring magazine 'Svensk Motortidning', the Postmaster-General, Julius Juhlin, discussed three possible means of solving "this particularly important problem".

The first was to use specially-built motor sleds. However, Juhlin did not foresee a promising future for this form of transport, since it could be used only when the road was completely covered with snow.

Another possibility was "to keep the roads open for automobiles by means of snowploughs"—a striking concept! Although he considered this the best solution, Juhlin also had reservations. While the approach might have been economically justifiable in built-up areas, it would not have been practical in sparsely-populated rural districts. And, as a further complication, the snow-ploughing vehicles themselves would have to be capable of overcoming the selfsame conditions.

The third alternative—and the one adopted by the Swedish Post Office—was to "build automobiles capable of negotiating snow-covered winter roads as well as summer roads, and of operating in thaw conditions".

The involvement of the Post Office in the problem must be seen in the light of its obligations to deliver mail and carry passengers in sparsely-populated regions. Because of this, it had a particular interest in developing a rational solution to the problem and to put its ideas into effect, it employed its own expert, Ernst Nyberg.

Aided by Juhlin's vision, Nyberg's inventiveness bore fruit in the form of fifteen functional post buses which were designed and

Above: Postmaster-General Julius Juhlin. Hugo Hamilton, Speaker of the Swedish parliament, is said to have remarked to him: "It is a shame that you did not introduce your excellent post bus service earlier. You might have saved the state the millions it spent building expensive railways through the Norrland wilderness."

The very first motor post bus ran between Lycksele and Tvärålund. Although the maiden trip at Christmas 1922 was successful, the first scheduled run on 1 January 1923 ended with the bus in a ditch with a broken skid.

built in close cooperation with Scania-Vabis in 1922–23.

The 36-hp engine drove the rear wheels through a four-speed gearbox, a propeller shaft and a double-reduction rear axle. This provided a total of eight speeds, the two lowest of which delivered extremely high traction. In addition, the other components were

somewhat over-designed to cope with the tough winter conditions.

Scania-Vabis built the chassis, which were then transported to the Post Office workshops at Ulvsunda for finishing of the vehicle under Ernst Nyberg's direction. Although an omnibus body was used, the interior layout could be varied to allow either one-third, two-thirds or the complete vehicle to be used for passengers (up to a maximum of twelve), with the remaining space for goods. A trailer for carrying goods and mail could be attached as required.

Two of Nyberg's inventions made the post bus unique. The first—track drive—was inspired by a Citroën desert vehicle, while the

second was a comfort feature boasted by few vehicles of the day; fresh air heated by the exhaust system was used to heat the passenger compartment. The idea became widely copied since Nyberg neglected to apply for a patent!

Impressive both for its ingenuity and performance, the track-drive feature is worthy of closer study. Two auxiliary rear axles (both fitted with pulleys) were installed, one in front and one behind the normal axle. These were easy to fit and remove as required by the conditions. Broad rubber tracks running around the rear wheels and the auxiliary pulleys afforded an excellent grip in snow, while the front wheels were also fitted with skids in winter. These measures reduced the ground loading dramatically, ensuring that the bus did not sink in loose snow.

Nyberg added other improvements. For example, the driver could adjust the auxiliary axles in the longitudinal and vertical directions to vary the tension of the tracks according to ground conditions. The problems had been overcome; not even a half-metre of fresh snow was sufficient to halt the progress of the bus.

The Post Office assumed a major role with the successful introduction of the post bus, as witnessed by the undertaking made by Julius Juhlin to the district medical office in Arjeplog:

"Should a sick person be in need of urgent transport to the hospital in Jörn, you need only telephone the postmaster there to request a bus. The postmaster has received or-

A functional workplace — a necessity when the blanket of snow extended for miles around. The powerful rear drive and front skids made the vehicle a trifle unpredictable! In particular, the side grip and the limited steering capability called for skill and anticipation on the part of the driver.

ders to place a vehicle immediately at the disposal of the patient in these circumstances, even if mail and passengers are delayed for a day". As though this were not enough, Juhlin went on to promise that "the patient will be charged the normal fare. The bus is heated and stout straw slippers are available".

One further step remained to be taken before the post bus achieved its final form. Although the novel drive ensured that the vehicles got through, progress was slow and fuel consumption was extremely high. In an attempt to overcome these problems, the experiment of mounting a snow-plough in front of the bus was tried during the winter of 1925–26. Clearing the road naturally facilitated progress, while the introduction of a more powerful engine enabled the tracks to be dispensed with. The solution proved satisfactory and the Post Office continued to exercise this function to some extent until 1947, when the roads administration was nationalised.

Clearing the northern roads of snow brought an unexpected disadvantage in the form of extra traffic by other vehicles, even private cars. The narrow tracks ploughed by the buses through the wilderness made every encounter an adventure. The choice was to keep a close eye on the timetable or to be prepared to shovel to get out of the way!

The post bus was instrumental in keeping the northern Swedish interior permanently open in winter, a remarkable achievement which was to be of major importance to the development of this remote area — not to mention the fact that tourists were quick to discover the attractions of travelling in comfort through the region.

SPECIFICATIONS	
Chassis	Type 3241
Wheelbase	3.44 m
Engine	Type II a (1441), 4-cylinder, side-valve carburettor unit
Output	36 hp
Bore	90 mm
Stroke	140 mm
Swept volume	3.56 litre
Bodybuilder	Postens Verkstäder
No. of passengers	12
No. built	6 (15)

Scania-Vabis 1927

—

'Noblesse'

THE 'VITESSE' WAS A classically elegant mahogany boat built in the late 1910s. Originally used by Scania-Vabis as a test craft and for entertaining prospective clients before the company's problems in the 1920s caused it to be sold, it is now owned by Rickard Bergström, who recovered it from its watery grave under a Stockholm bridge and carried out a superb job of renovation.

The same Rickard Bergström was also responsible for transforming a broken-down 1927 post and military field-post bus into the unique vehicle which Scania has been using almost daily since the mid-80s as a VIP transport at its Södertälje plant. The bus proudly bears the name 'Noblesse'.

The connection between the two is obvious; both feature the same luxurious mahogany and plush interior, and are finished with the same precision and attention to detail. Without doubt the only vehicle of its type in the world, 'Noblesse' is both enjoyable to ride in and attractive to the eye. Although none of the interior details is original, the body is the one built by ASJ in Linköping when the vehicle was refitted in 1935. At the same time, the wheelbase was increased to 5.25 m.

Supplied originally to the Swedish Post Office in 1927 for service in the province of Jämtland, the bus was actually of the same type as the post buses described on page 46 and was rebuilt in 1935 to double the number

The elegant mahogany and plush interior of 'Noblesse' is an example of craftsmanship of the highest order.

of passengers from fourteen to twenty-eight. 'Called up' in 1939, it was used by the military as a field-post bus. Bought back by Scania-Vabis in 1959, it was rebuilt in 1981–83 and fitted with the elegant interior which now accommodates ten passengers in style.

Two veteran beauties: 'Vitesse' and 'Noblesse' pictured together at Djurgården in Stockholm.

	SPECIFICATIONS
Chassis	Type 3243
Wheelbase	3.70 m
Engine	Type 1461, 6-cylinder, OHV carburettor unit
Output	75 hp
Swept volume	5.78 litre
Bodybuilder	Scania-Vabis
Passengers	14 seated
No. built	7

SCANIA-VABIS'S SUCCESSFUL COLLABORA-
TION with the Swedish Post Office in developing the post bus had demonstrated its
ability and readiness to solve special transport problems. To some extent, this was a
matter of survival following the cutbacks necessitated by the acute financial problems
of the early 1920s. Managing Director Gunnar Lindmark and Chief Design Engineer
August Nilsson were the men who piloted

Scania-Vabis
1925

———

*SJ's
seventh bus*

Scania-Vabis successfully through the decade.

However, the company's position in the
market had been tenuous from the very beginning. Not only was the car and light-truck
sector swamped by cheap imports, but truck
and car chassis were also being used to build
buses. To attempt to compete in this 'hot-
house' climate would have been foolhardy in
the opinion of company management.

A letter-box (costing 90 crowns) was built into the side of the body beside the driver's seat.

During this period, Scania-Vabis developed a series of new engines which took the market by storm and quickly won a reputation for durability, long life and economy. From then on, engine technology was to make a major contribution to Scania-Vabis' competitiveness—as indeed it does to this day.

The explosive growth of the bus market in the latter half of the 1920s was completely unforeseen. However, Lindmark and Nilsson not only succeeded in keeping abreast of developments, but even contrived to lead the field in some respects. The new bus with progressive springing, which was introduced in 1923, was much appreciated by operators and passengers alike. Its smoother running ensured that far fewer components shook loose and caused problems while, for the first time, the ride was genuinely comfortable.

The manufacture of trucks and buses had now been coordinated to the extent that the drive train components were common.

A major new customer—Swedish State Railways, or SJ—was now monitoring developments in the bus market with the greatest interest. Despite its title, SJ had been operating a small number of bus services, mainly in rural areas not served by rail traffic, since 1911. Although its fleet consisted exclusively of imported makes (including Daimler, Mercedes and MAN), Scania-Vabis now offered so many attractive features that SJ decided to test its capabilities by 'buying Swedish' and placing the order for its seventh bus with the company.

It was the beginning of a huge growth in provincial bus services by independent operators as well as SJ. All over the country, the bus quickly became an efficient and versatile complement to the railway.

SJ's seventh bus was this Scania-Vabis 3752 delivered on 8 July 1925. After serving in Bohuslän for fifteen years, it became part of SJ's collection of veteran buses and was presented to Scania-Vabis on the occasion of the company's 75th anniversary in 1966. Completely restored, it is now in the Scania Museum.

As an alternative, it was decided to discontinue car production in 1925, while concentrating seriously on a new generation of heavy trucks (over 2 tonnes), a sector in which the company had better prospects of establishing itself. 'The Fast Truck' was a success, while the manufacture of cars ceased at almost the appointed time, the very last models being built in 1929 (see page 60).

SPECIFICATIONS	
Chassis	Type 3752
Wheelbase	4.56 m
Overall length	6.70 m
Gross weight	5,960 kg
Engine	Type III (1546), 4-cylinder, side-valve carburettor unit
Output	50 hp
Swept volume	5.03 litre
Bodybuilder	Leonard Jansson Karosserifabrik, Stockholm
No. of passengers	24 seated
No. built	20 (38)

IN THE LATE 1920S, brewery director Sten
Simonsson of Södertälje and Scania-Vabis
MD Per Lindmark were frequent fellow passengers on the train between Södertälje and
Stockholm, and the agreement for the
supply of a new 2.5-tonne truck (Type 3251)
to the brewery is said to have been concluded
on one of these occasions.

In those days, even relatively small towns

Scania-Vabis
1927

'The Fast Truck'

had their own breweries. The brewing industry in Södertälje dated from the mid-1800s
and, by 1927, Södertälje Bryggeri had about
forty employees and a fleet of six trucks.

The new acquisition was used initially to
transport raw materials to the brewery from
barges in Södertälje port. Some years later,
it became a delivery truck, operating within
a 50-kilometre radius—something of a haz-

registered at the end of 1950, the truck had covered approximately 800,000 kilometres. Presented to Scania-Vabis by Pripps (the brewing concern) in 1965, it became something of a celebrity in the vintage car world as the first Swedish entry in the classic London to Brighton Rally for commercial vehicles in 1967.

Since Scania-Vabis was, at that time, making strenuous efforts to enter the British market with its new LB76 (see page 96), the truck was kept in England for several months before returning to Sweden with a series of trophies from several veteran rallies. In the London to Brighton event, it won the prize for the vehicle which had travelled furthest to reach the starting line under its own steam.

In 1925, Scania-Vabis introduced a completely new truck chassis together with a new type of engine with a combined gearbox. Twice as fast as its chain-driven counterparts, the model was described in company advertisements as 'The Fast Truck'.

The 'brewery' truck (one of several versions built) is a typical representative of this type.

ardous operation at a time when drivers were allowed free beer...

Like so many others, the truck was converted to run on producer gas during the Second World War, while fuel shortages also created problems during the postwar years. (In 1947–48, strict rationing even forced the brewery to resort to horse-drawn transport to make deliveries.) By the time it was de-

SPECIFICATIONS	
Chassis	Type 3251
Wheelbase	3.70 m
Engine	Type 1544, 4-cylinder, OHV carburettor unit
Output	50 hp
Swept volume	4.27 litre
Superstructure	Rigid platform
Payload	2,480 kg
No. built	190 (218)

Scania-Vabis 1928

*After fifty years on the bottom,
the 'Fryken' truck again runs
like a watch!*

On 27 FEBRUARY 1936, driver Sven Ljungqvist and his helper, Axel Bredsberg, were
clearing a track for trotting races to be held
on icebound Lake Fryken at Genvägen, near
Svenneby. As usual, the oval track had been
staked out and marked prior to clearing with
the 'Lycksele' snowplough with which their
Scania truck was fitted. All that remained
was to clear a path in the centre for the
officials.

Then, disaster struck as the truck ran into
an opening in the ice about 100 metres from
shore and started to sink, rear-end first.
Luckily, both occupants were able to
scramble clear onto solid ice, but not before
Sven Ljungqvist's overcoat and lunchbox, together with a new gramophone record, disappeared into the depths.

The water was deep indeed! When the
lake was dragged immediately afterwards in
the vicinity of the accident, the depth on the
shore side of the opening was found to be 35
metres and that at the outer edge twice as
much. All attempts to recover the truck were
abandoned after a week and S5406 was con-
signed to the deep forever. Close by, however,
was a rock projecting above the surface of the
lake—and Sven Ljungqvist was one of those
who remembered its position.

Not until 1979 was the possibility of rais-
ing the sunken truck again seriously discussed. Nothing more happened until spring
1982 when the Nordvärmland Veteran Car
Club appointed a salvage committee to un-

Cleaning, valve-grinding and
minor adjustments were all
that were needed to make the
engine of the 'Fryken' truck
run again after more than a
half-century on the floor of
Lake Fryken.

dertake the task. The committee's first step
was to interview Sven Ljungqvist to ascer-
tain the position of the rock said to indicate
the location. Unable to locate it, the committee assumed that the rock was now below
water level. Turning to more scientific meth-
ods, soundings were taken to locate the underwater precipice said by Ljungqvist to be

situated about 85 metres from shore. After a comprehensive series of tests, the experts were reasonably sure of its location. And the reason for their previous failure to locate the rock became clear at low tide; it was now concealed by a concrete pier.

Further dragging was carried out in summer 1982 and the general location of the

The 'Fryken' truck was equipped with a three-way hydraulic tipper and electric windscreen wipers. A right-hand drive model, it was fitted with single rear wheels for winter service using a 'Lycksele' snowplough.

truck was established. The following summer, diver Lasse Eriksson from Stockholm reached a depth of 67 metres at the two points which had been marked by buoys, but was unable to leave his descent line to search for the vehicle.

At this juncture, Karlstad Sub-Aqua Club recommended that special underwater TV equipment be hired from the firm of Under-vattensfoto in Sollentuna. Although the equipment was used for two days in June 1984, efforts to find the truck were unsuccessful.

Anders Liljestrand from Gothenburg, an expert in underwater detection by magnetometer, led a fresh attempt the following September. The indications proved positive and, at 19.32 hours on 29 September 1984, the location of the 'Fryken' truck was finally pinpointed.

Salvage work was scheduled to commence in early summer 1985, the lift to be carried out by two powerful cable winches mounted on a large pontoon. It was destined to be a difficult operation. The pontoon broke up during the winter, necessitating major repairs, and by the time these were completed, SKr17,000 had already been expended on the project, in addition to an enormous number of manhours.

The lift was to be carried out in two stages. The plan was to raise the truck initially to just below the surface and move it to shallower water, where it could be suspended under the pontoon for transport to Oleby Quay in Torsby. There, it would again be lowered into the water prior to final recovery. In the event, what appeared on paper to be a simple operation actually took several arduous weeks to accomplish.

A pair of hooks, made especially for the first lift, were to be attached to the truck with the aid of the TV camera. However, with the hooks in position, it was found that the winch cables were too light to raise the vehicle which, by now, was firmly embedded in the mud. As bad luck would have it, one of the cables broke and became entangled with the truck and camera, preventing the latter from being raised. Since the camera was

Complete with snowchains and plough, the 'Fryken' truck reappears in its natural element after half a century under Lake Fryken.

The simple, yet functional, instrumentation included a clock, oil-pressure gauge, ammeter and speedometer (with odometer). The variable panel-lighting control is at top centre, with the ignition switch and light switch underneath.

worth SKr150,000, many sighs of relief were heaved when it was eventually recovered after several tension-filled weeks....

Despite the problems, the truck at last was suspended in shallow water off Genvägen, near Svenneby, at midnight on Thursday, 4 July, ready for transport to Oleby Quay in preparation for the final lift on Sunday, 21 July 1985.

Whatever the Veteran Car Club members had expected, they was clearly taken by surprise by the interest shown in the operation. About thirty vintage vehicles were present, accompanied by 3,000 or so paying spectators. To applause from the large crowd and the sounding of its contemporaries' horns, the 'Fryken' truck finally emerged from the waters of the lake into the light of day, after spending half a century among the sunken timbers and other debris on the muddy bottom.

SPECIFICATIONS	
Chassis	Type 3256
Wheelbase	3.80 m
Gross weight	5,850 kg
Engine	Type 1544, 4-cylinder, OHV carburettor unit
Output	50 hp
Swept volume	4.27 litre
Superstructure	Platform with 3-way tipper
Payload	3,000 kg
No. built	39 (41)

IN FEBRUARY 1956, BIL och Buss, the Scania and Volkswagen dealers in Gävle, received a letter from Lassar-Emil Olsson in Limedsforsen. Including an order for 675 crown's worth of spares for the truck supplied to him in October 1929, the letter read: "I would not spend this amount of money on an old truck were the new models not too large and cumbersome for my purposes. Furthermore, since any make other than Scania-Vabis is out of the question, I intend to hold on to my old truck. It has now been running for twenty-six years with no breakdowns apart from a broken rear axle. The engine itself is still going strong and has been the epitome of reliability."

Lassar-Emil was certainly not of the 'use it and scrap it' school—he had bought himself a reliable product and had taken good care of it. His Scania-Vabis had cost over SKr17,000, and no expense had been spared on tools and accessories. Lassar-Emil ran a forge together with his brother, Johan, a technically-gifted individual who had never bothered to apply for a driving licence. One of the brothers' products was the 'Lassar' snowplough of their own design. ('Lassar', the

Scania-Vabis 1929

'Lassar-Emil's' truck passed inspection in 1974 after 1,500,000 kilometres on the road!

SPECIFICATIONS	
Chassis	Type 3244
Wheelbase	3.80 m
Engine	Type 1561, 6-cylinder, OHV carburettor unit
Output	85 hp
Swept volume	6.42 litre
Payload	3,000 kg
No. built	126 (269)

name of their farm, was used as a prefix in the manner typical of the Dalarna region in which they lived.)

In winter, the truck was used to demonstrate the snowplough to prospective customers around the country, and also had the task of clearing the roads in the Lima district during the normally long, snowy winters. In addition, the vehicle was used for transporting timber and gravel.

Having taken delivery of his spares in 1956, Lassar-Emil continued to use his truck on the narrow Dalarna roads right up to 1974. By this time, it had covered approximately 1,500,000 kilometres, passing its annual official inspection without difficulty.

Lassar-Emil continued to correspond with his dealers. In a letter written in 1961 he remarked: "Since the truck is intended to become part of Scania's proposed museum, I shall continue to maintain it in such order that it starts first time, be it 50 or 100 years hence."

And indeed, 'Lassar-Emil's' truck is now in the Scania Museum—still starting first time, just as he intended!

AFTER AN INITIAL ATTEMPT to launch a motor-omnibus service in 1899 (using a German vehicle), it was to be another twenty years before motor-driven buses again appeared on the streets of Stockholm.

At the time, the city centre was served by a tramway network which was so comprehensive that buses were considered unnecessary. Furthermore, although several applications were submitted during the 1910s, the municipal authorities had a vested interest in the tramways and blocked all proposals to grant rights to competitive forms of transport.

Meanwhile, the suburbs were proving a goldmine for the operators, and omnibus companies (many of whom operated services as far as the city limits, where the trams took over) were springing up everywhere under licences granted by the Stockholm Governor's office. In addition to a driving licence, drivers were required to comply with certain regulations pertaining to commercial traffic.

By mid-1923, 81 buses were estimated to be serving twenty-four routes between the capital and its suburbs, while a further 150 to 200 were being used to operate regular services in the county. Both the quality of the service and the vehicles themselves varied greatly, the latter including everything from Model T Fords with platform-mounted benches to vehicles with purpose-built chassis. Some of the services were short-lived, whereas others became highly successful. Among the latter was the Huvudsta-Stockholm line, which carried no less than 1,001,582 passengers in 1923.

Even greater numbers of applications to operate city-centre bus services were made in the early 1920s, by which time both the city authorities and the tramway company had realised the wisdom of establishing a more comprehensive city network. It was decided that the entire matter merited detailed study.

By early 1921, the authorities had reached the stage of pronouncing that trams were the preferable form of transport, partly on the grounds that they carried more passengers and followed a fixed track, whereas buses were not subject to this restriction. Their deliberations reached a conclusion on 29 September 1922 when one H. von Kraemer was finally granted an operating licence.

On 23 July 1923, Stockholms Centrala

Scania-Vabis 1928

The '54'

The '54' boasted an attractive and functional interior with a bench seat along the left-hand side and double seats on the right. Passengers entered at the rear and alighted at the driver's end. The body was generously provided with windows, while the complete vehicle gave a solid and reliable impression.

Omnibus AB (SCO) commenced services using eleven Vulcans, a British model built on a truck chassis. Operations proved profitable, prompting Stockholm Tramways (SS) to acquire shares in the company in 1925. Four years later, to avert the bankruptcy of SCO, SS took over all its operating licences, assets and liabilities, bringing all the passenger-transport services in central Stockholm under a single umbrella.

Passenger numbers grew enormously as the network was expanded. SCO carried more than 17 million passengers in 1928.

SCO acquired its first four Scania-Vabis buses in 1925. The pace of delivery quickened during the next few years, and no less

than thirty Type 8404 models were purchased between 1926 and 1928. Nicknamed the 'Racer' because of its advanced performance, this model was powered by a modern four-cylinder, OHV, 60-hp engine. (In this context, it should be noted that the buses were limited to a speed of 20 km/h until 1931.)

However, the 1928 model pictured above is a Type 8406, a somewhat larger variant of its predecessor, the 8404. Among its new features, the 8406 numbered a completely new six-cylinder engine and a Bosch brake servo.

The '54' was typical of the bonneted models built by Scania-Vabis. Although the buses were completely modern in mechani-

A genuine treasure, the '54' has been presented to the Scania Museum by the SL Tramway Museum.

cal terms, body design was to undergo major development over the next few years.

SPECIFICATIONS	
Chassis	Type 8406
Wheelbase	5.25 m
Overall length	8.35 m
Gross weight	7,965 kg
Engine	Type 1461, six-cylinder, OHV carburettor unit
Output	75 hp
Bore	95 mm
Stroke	136 mm
Swept volume	5.78 litre
Bodybuilder	AB Arvika Vagnfabrik
No. of passengers	24 seated, 16 standing
No. built	60 (188)

BY THE END OF the 1920s, car production at Scania-Vabis was no more than a memory. As part of the comprehensive modernisation programme undertaken by the new company management following the enforced liquidation of the original Scania-Vabis in 1921, it was decided that the activity would be discontinued in 1925. However, use was made of those parts and components which had already been manufactured, and a further 52 vehicles were built between 1926 and 1929 when the book finally closed on the car era. Including the Erikson car, production

Scania-Vabis limousine 1929

The last car

totalled approximately 830 cars and other vehicles built on car chassis. The very last of the cars is the subject of this article.

The year was 1929, and it had been decided to build a further two cars, not for sale but for company use. Since Scania-Vabis had a sales office in Stockholm, Managing Director Gunnar Lindmark considered it proper that the company should continue to use its own make of car as long as possible.

Similar in appearance, the two models were built as open phaetons, but with a permanent superstructure.

Above: The 1929 at the start of renovation work. The car was stripped completely, all the body components ground and the model painstakingly reassembled. New parts were made to replace the many original components which were unusable. The total cost of refurbishment is estimated to have exceeded SKr100,000, not including labour.

registered on 11 February 1949. It continued to travel the roads of Uppland province until 1954 and was resold to Scania three years later for the sum of SKr3,000. Now, following its return to its 'birthplace' in Södertälje, it has been refurbished in time for the centenary celebrations.

An interesting construction, the last car might aptly be called a 'spare parts' model, since most of its components were actually surplus parts from the stores. Although based on a Type I chassis of the same type as the 'Nyblin' car described on page 36 and the 'Kälarne' car (page 41), it was somewhat longer than the original type and had a modified suspension. The 1929 car was a four-door model with a covered body which was built only for it and its companion (the Type I was normally built as a phaeton). Unlike the Type I, the gear lever was centrally located rather than outside the body on the right-hand side.

Appropriately, the 1929 car also had an unusual engine—a modified Type I unit equipped with overhead valves and designated the 1347.

The last to be built was based in Stockholm, where it was in the care of Nils Landberg, the office general factotum. Given the chance of buying the car when it was replaced a few years later, Landberg seized the opportunity and, as owner, sold it—without tyres—to Edvin Segerman of Riala for 360 crowns on 16 February 1943. (Segerman was a haulier who had become acquainted with Nils Landberg in the course of his dealings with the head office.) The car was taken out of mothballs in 1948 when tyres again became available after the war and was re-

Originally, the car was finished in sand beige with a darker top section and black wings. Later, Segerman repainted the entire vehicle chocolate brown. The finish of the restored car is the same as when it emerged from the factory sixty years ago.

SPECIFICATIONS	
Chassis	Type 2122 (modified Type I)
Engine	Type 1347, 4-cylinder, OHV carburettor unit
Output	35 hp
Swept volume	2.32 litre
Body	Four-door covered body for 5 occupants
No. built	2

1930–1939

*During the decade, Scania-Vabis achieved
a higher profile as a bus manufacturer, producing 1,602
buses and 970 trucks. Among other factors, this growth
was due to the introduction of the new forward-control
'Bulldog' bus. Superseded in the 1930s, first by the
Hesselman engine and later by a pure diesel, petrol
engines were on the way out. Meanwhile, production of
producer-gas engines was undertaken towards the end of
the decade, as the impending war threatened Swedish
fuel supplies. In the first five decades of its existence,
the company had manufactured 830 car chassis,
2,614 trucks, 2,032 buses and 1,340 separate engines.*

Scania-Vabis 1932

—

The 'Bulldog'

AUGUST NILSSON LITTLE REALISED how popular his ingenious design was to become. As chief designer at Scania-Vabis throughout the interwar years, he was responsible for a series of striking innovations which had a profound impact on the company's development. Among other factors, the days of the bonneted vehicle were numbered.

The demand for larger buses grew as bus traffic increased during the 1920s. However, the maximum permissible rear-axle weight was an obstacle to development, since a larger body inevitably increased the load on the rear wheels, threatening to exceed the 4-tonne limit imposed by the legislators. On the other hand, it was difficult to utilise the permissible front-axle weight fully in the bonneted type of vehicle.

Buses which differed essentially from their truck-based ancestors now began to appear—a development initiated by Stockholm Tramways which, in 1928, imported a Leyland Tiger from London to study the novel British solution to the location of the driver's compartment. Adopting the concept immediately, Tidaholms Bruk became the first Swedish manufacturer to build a copy of the Leyland model. Moving the driver's seat towards the front not only served to increase the front-axle weight but—more importantly—allowed the entire compartment to the rear of the engine to be used as passenger accommodation, while providing space for two extra seats. Scania-Vabis and Nohab followed quickly, and between 1929 and 1935, all buses ordered by public transport utilities in Stockholm were of the new design.

The Scania-Vabis 'Bulldog' was characterised by simple and harmonious, even natural lines. Utilising every available centimetre and kilogramme, the simplicity of its design made it revolutionary. The model shown (a Type 8307) was delivered in July 1932 to Mölnlycke Bil & Omnibus AB.

However, neither August Nilsson nor the Scania-Vabis management was satisfied with progress. News that American manufacturers were building buses with a completely flat front had reached their ears and, since they were well aware of the advantages offered by this type of body in terms of capacity, Managing Director Gunnar Lindmark, accompanied by Nilsson, journeyed west in 1929 to see this somewhat revolutionary development at first hand. Meanwhile, Swedish speed and axle-weight restrictions had been eased, increasing the attractions of large buses.

Among other models, the two viewed the Twin Coach, a bus with a full-length body overhung at the front and powered by twin engines—one driving each rear wheel! Duly impressed, they actually succeeded in negotiating the manufacturing rights for the model in northern Europe.

The Scania-Vabis Type 1564 six-cylinder engine was unusually narrow. A more 'normal' engine would have required modification to provide space for the driver, power unit and passengers at the front of the 'Bulldog' bus.

Although the Twin Coach was never actually built in Sweden, August Nilsson used it as a basis for further innovation. Both he and his engineering colleagues were apprehensive of the problems which the twin engines might pose. Ensuring that both delivered the same traction would be difficult, not to mention the handling problems which might be experienced on icy winter roads. Furthermore, since none of Scania-Vabis's standard components could be used in the construction, the vehicle would be extremely costly.

The ingeniously simple solution was to locate the engine inside the passenger compartment—something which might appear self-evident nowadays, but which was far from obvious at the time. As a further innovation, the body was overhung ahead of the front wheels and the engine was relocated above, rather than behind, the front axle, enabling the designers to make full use of the permissible front-axle weight without modifying the fundamental design. Compared with the Twin Coach, the construction was breathtakingly simple.

The first example of the new Scania-Vabis bus (Type 8305) entered service between the Mälaren islands, near Stockholm, in January 1932, followed in April by the Type 8307 (which was 5 cm wider). The model was an immediate success. Extremely spacious for its length and wheelbase, no less than fifty-five were sold by year's end.

Nicknamed the 'Bulldog' by the public (a title which was quickly adopted by Scania-Vabis and the rest of the industry), the type signified the breakthrough of the full forward-control bus—a concept which is universal today.

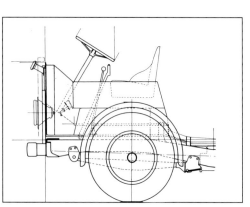

The higher front-axle weight (now almost double) resulted in unavoidably high steering forces. Redesign of the entire front-end geometry and suspension was needed to reduce these to acceptable levels.

SPECIFICATIONS	
Chassis	Type 8307
Wheelbase	4.90 m
Overall length	8.45 m
Gross weight	9,250 kg
Engine	Type 1564, 6-cylinder, OHV carburettor unit
Output	100 hp
Swept volume	6.4 litre
Bodybuilder	Svenska Maskinverken
No. of passengers	36 seated, 8 standing
No. built	34 (101)

MANY OF THE TRUCKS built by Scania-Vabis in the 1930s were supplied to roads administrations and private firms engaged in road-maintenance, snow-ploughing and similar activities. One of these was a vehicle familiarly known as 'Sörsjön' after the Dalarna townland in which its owner, Ivar D. Mattsson, lived. Delivered in October 1934, the truck was one of eighty-two produced by Scania-Vabis that year.

Originally powered by a Type 1566, 80-hp Hesselman engine with a bore of 105 mm, the vehicle was run on producer gas throughout the Second World War. When fuel oil again became available, the truck was equipped with a new power unit (Type 16621, also a Hesselman) with a 110-mm bore.

Used mainly for snow-ploughing on mountain roads, the vehicle was fitted with single rear wheels with size 900–20 tyres, a configuration offering much better mobility than the original specification of 750–20 tyres all round and twin wheels at the rear.

The 'Sörsjön' truck was a true workhorse. Perhaps it had been 'infected' by 'Lassar-Emil's' 1929 truck (page 57) just a few kilometres away! In fact, the two were sometimes used in tandem to provide extra power

Scania-Vabis 1934

"Unique ruggedness and durability"

SPECIFICATIONS	
Chassis	Type 3352
Wheelbase	3.80 m
Gross weight	6,580 kg
Engine	Type 1566, 6-cylinder Hesselman unit
Output	80 hp
Swept volume	7.07 litre
Payload	2,360 kg
No. built	15 (113)

under particularly heavy snow conditions.

Ivar Mattsson's impressions of his work and his truck are described in a letter written, in 1954, to Egon Ardelius, then technical director of Scania-Vabis, Södertälje—and the dealer who had sold the truck to Mattsson in Dalarna twenty years earlier! "In my opinion, the truck is unique for its ruggedness and durability, despite the severe conditions under which it has been used. During the first ten years of its life, it was used to transport heavy loads of timber, hauling a trailer and usually working double shifts. Later on, it was fitted with a plough for clearing two metres (sometimes more) of snow from mountain roads. In summer, it was fitted with a bulldozer blade and used to load gravel."

The vehicle had covered about 1,450,000 kilometres in this type of service by the time it was bought by Scania-Vabis in 1957.

Scania-Vabis 8422 1936–1944

A classic 'bulldog' chassis powered by Scania-Vabis's first diesel

UNTIL TRAFFIC MOVEMENTS WERE restricted during the Second World War, the method of 'delivering' Scania-Vabis bus chassis throughout Sweden—in summer or winter—was for the customer to collect his vehicle at the plant and drive it to the coachbuilder's premises under its own steam.

The vehicle pictured above is a 1939 Type 8422/4 bus chassis which was collected in Södertälje and driven to the works of Hägglund & Söner in Örnsköldsvik—a 15-hour journey—in the depths of winter. The bus was sold by the Scania-Vabis dealer in Sundsvall to local operators Biltrafik Aktiebolaget Njurunda.

During the next eleven years, the bus covered approximately 700,000 kilometres in scheduled service on the Sundsvall-Njurunda-Skatan route, burning producer gas dur-

ing the war years. On occasion, it was equipped with a twin-axle passenger trailer to increase its capacity.

Following its retirement, the bus was used as a mobile rest room, ending up in a quarry outside Gnarp, just south of Sundsvall, where it was discovered in 1977 by Sture Gottvall, whose father had sold it years before. Sture is pictured above driving the newly-renovated chassis, just as in the 1930s when he helped his father to collect chassis from the Scania-Vabis works.

Type 8422 was powered by a precombustion-chamber diesel engine – the first 'true' Scania-Vabis diesel, which was introduced in 1936. This had been preceded, in 1932, by the Hesselman engine (which was built under licence), a unit which burned crude oil but was started with petrol. However, the

Writing in the June 1936 issue of the Swedish trade journal, 'Svensk Omnibustidning', John Nerén described a test drive in a Scania-Vabis bus powered by the new diesel as follows: "To my surprise, I could hardly hear the engine. However, I certainly felt its effect—the bus shot forward like an arrow from the bow when moving off from stops or when overtaking slow-moving trucks."

simple working principle and efficiency of the diesel appealed more to August Nilsson, Scania-Vabis's chief engineer.

Although Rudolf Diesel's original patent dated from 1893, his engine was, for many years, far too bulky for widespread use in vehicles; apart from its size and weight, the problems of speed control and noise were difficult to overcome. Nonetheless, August Nilsson discovered that Magirus was manufacturing relatively smooth-running diesels in Germany, and Scania-Vabis acquired the technical support necessary to build its own precombustion version by concluding a licensing agreement with that firm.

As with the preceding generation of engines, it was essential that the width of the

This bus with a Type 8422 chassis was delivered, in 1939, to the Malmö Tramway Company. The coachbuilders were Svenska Karosseriverkstäderna, who were subsequently taken over by Scania. In 1967, the model was presented to Svenska Spårvägs Sällskapet (the Swedish Tramway Society).

unit should not create a problem in the limited space available in a 'bulldog' model. Consequently, the design was, of necessity, extremely compact, while the weight was reduced by making components such as the pistons, intake manifold, covers and crankcase of silumin (an aluminium alloy). Noise and vibration were reduced by installing purpose-designed rubber mountings, while both the crankshaft and propeller shaft were fitted with vibration dampers.

The new engine quickly won appreciation for its reliability and running economy. The same basic engine was also available in petrol and Hesselman versions, although the latter was quickly superseded by the diesel. All units were convertible, at reasonable cost, to burn the other fuels—a facility which was to prove extremely useful during the coming war years.

The diesel developed 120 hp compared with the 135 hp of the petrol version. The Scania-Vabis engineers had mastered the problems and developed a notable power source for heavy vehicles.

The engine was extremely compact in both width and length. (Observers noted that it was the same physical size as a 5-litre engine.) The oil pressure warning lamp was a new feature in this type of vehicle. The plate read: "Lamp will light when oil pressure is low and when engine is stopped."

SPECIFICATIONS	
Chassis	Type 8422/4
Wheelbase	5.00 m
Engine	Type 16641, 6-cylinder precombustion-chamber diesel
Output	120 hp
Swept volume	7.75 litre
No. built	47 (262)

1940–1949

At the outbreak of war in 1939, Scania-Vabis's was producing 300 vehicles per year. By the time peace dawned, this had been multiplied several times over by a succession of major defence orders (totalling 1,037 vehicles) and by a programme of expansion implemented despite wartime difficulties. During the decade, the company became general agent in Sweden for both Volkswagen and Willys Overland, and the national dealer network was expanded. Export sales were also beginning to grow. Vehicle production exceeded 1,000 for the first time in 1946, while 1947 was the last year in which buses were built in greater numbers than trucks. Beginning the decade with 940 employees, the company ended it with over 2,000.

THE SWEDISH TRUCK POPULATION was dominated by petrol-driven models at the start of the Second World War, and traffic was completely dependent on fuel supplies from abroad. Since the use of imported fuel was severely restricted, measures were taken to convert to domestic fuels and to introduce alternative forms of transport. Meanwhile, with the almost immediate introduction of petrol rationing on 1 September 1939, long-haul trucks were given supplies only in exceptional cases.

With the German occupation of Denmark and Norway, and the ensuing blockade of the Skagerrak in April 1940, imports of fuel to Sweden were halted and the entire nation was mobilised. All long-haul traffic was diverted to the railways, while the horse and bicycle again came into their own. Producer gas became the only means of keeping trucks on the road, the government providing subsidies for the purchase of the necessary units.

In 1938, before the crisis, the Royal Swedish Academy of Engineering Sciences had been appointed by the government to examine the feasibility of using charcoal gas as an automotive fuel, and several Swedish engineers were already working on the development of a producer-gas unit. Axel Svedlund, an Örebro engineer and pioneer in the field, developed an all-Swedish unit which was destined to become one of the most popular. Unlike its foreign counterparts (such as the Imbert unit), which were fired with wood blocks, the Svedlund unit was fired with charcoal.

No less than 16,000 trucks were converted to producer-gas operation between April and November 1940. All petrol distribution ceased on 1 December and the number of gas-driven vehicles increased rapidly, reaching 31,000 by 31 May 1941 and almost 35,000, or over 90% of the total truck population, in 1942.

At the outbreak of the war, Scania-Vabis was in the throes of changing to diesel production. Having built the first diesel of its own design in 1936, the company was now manufacturing its four, six and eight-cylinder 'unitary' engines (designated the D400, D600 and D800 respectively). These were now to be converted to run on producer gas.

In 1941, the company built a number of heavy Type 33500 gas-driven trucks

Scania-Vabis Type 33520 1941

Producer gas-driven tractor unit

Producer gas became the alternative wartime fuel. Delivered to Hellefors Bruk, this Type 33520 tractor (fitted with the original Scania-Vabis cab) was powered by an eight-cylinder diesel engine with an Imbert gas generator installed behind the cab. Although heavy and cumbersome, the unit was reliable and cheap to run.

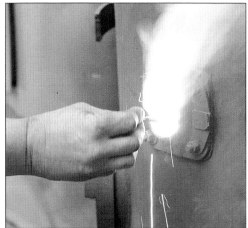

equipped with 10.34-litre, eight-cylinder in-line unitary engines designed to burn petrol, light bentyl or diesel oil. Due to the lower calorific value of the gas, the output was only 120 hp compared with the normal 180 hp. (Light bentyl was another wartime fuel consisting of 75% petrol and 25% motor spirit.)

Delivered to Hellefors Bruk, one of these 10-tonne Scania-Vabis trucks was also the first to be equipped with a unitary engine. The vehicle was a typical heavy tractor unit of the day, with a sloping radiator in front of a long bonnet and an original Scania-Vabis cab. The fuel source was an Imbert wood-gas generator (the type which was used predominantly in heavy trucks during the latter years of the war) installed behind the cab, with its own cooler in front of the ordinary radiator. Twelve eight-cylinder producer-gas trucks (including six Type 33520 models) were built in 1941 and 1942.

SPECIFICATIONS	
Chassis	Type 33520/1
Wheelbase	4.10 m
Gross weight	10,000 kg
Engine	Type B801, 8-cylinder carburettor unit (modified to burn producer gas)
Output	Approx. 120 hp
Bore	110 mm
Stroke	136 mm
Swept volume	10.34 litre
Max. load	4,850 kg
No. built	6

SKP m/42
1943–1946

SAV m/43
1944–1947

Two armoured vehicles built for the Swedish army. The SKP will continue in service until the next century

As the necessity of modernising and strengthening the Swedish Defence Forces became apparent during the emergency years, Scania-Vabis received orders for vehicles of several types.

In 1941, the army ordered an armoured car as a transport for tank support infantry. Although the vehicle was to be equipped with a special armour-plated body, it was also to be built on a truck chassis.

Scania-Vabis based the design on its four-wheel drive, cross-country F11–0 truck chassis, which had also been built for the military. This was used to construct a prototype SKP vehicle, in which 'S' stood for Scania-Vabis, 'K' for 'kaross' (the Swedish for 'body') and 'P' for 'pansar' (meaning 'armoured').

The armour plating provided protection for two men in the driver's seat and eleven troops in the open (unroofed) rear. Production commenced in late 1943 and no less than 262 SKPs were built within the next three years.

General George Patton, the legendary leader of the US armoured forces, was impressed by the SKP when he saw it at Strängnäs in 1945, praising the Swedes for having successfully built such an efficient vehicle with minimal resources.

The SKP also served as an essential part of the Swedish UN Forces' armoury in the Belgian Congo in 1960–64. Veterans of that campaign recall the versatile role which it played in action against the Baluba tribe and against the rebel forces of Moise Tshombe in breakaway Katanga.

The SKP proved to be long-lived. In the mid-1950s, it was equipped with improved weaponry and, in 1971, with a newly de-

signed braking system. Further modernisation was undertaken about ten years later when, at the instigation of the Gotland command, the vehicle was equipped with a roof, a shorter rear section with a door, low-profile tyres, single rear wheels and superior armament. However, it is still powered by the original Scania-Vabis 402, four-cylinder, 115-hp petrol engine, while the main gearbox (a four-speed non-synchromesh unit with a two-speed auxiliary box) has also survived from the 1940s.

SPECIFICATIONS

Armoured vehicle	Type SKP m/42	Type SAV m/41
Chassis	F11–01	Type m/41 tank
Overall length	6.90 m	4.61 m
Gross weight	8,500 kg	11,700 kg
Engine	Type 402/1, 4-cyl. carburettor unit	Type 603/2, 6-cyl. carburettor unit
Output	115 hp	160 hp
Bore	115 mm	115 mm
Stroke	136 mm	136 mm
Swept volume	5.65 litre	8.47 litre
Number of crew	2+13	4
Armament	Machine gun	75/105-mm cannon
No. built	262	36

The army commissioned Scania-Vabis to modify a prototype m/41 tank to carry a 75-mm cannon. (A 105-mm weapon was installed later.) Costing SKr36,000, the project was a success and, in March 1944, a contract was signed for the supply of eighteen SAV m/43 vehicles (as the type was then known). These were delivered between November 1944 and January 1945.

A further eighteen SAVs were ordered towards the end of 1945. Like the first series, these were based on the m/41 tank chassis, the origin of which was interesting. Ninety of these had been ordered by the Swedish army from the Czech manufacturers in 1940 but delivery had been blocked by the Germans, then in occupation of Czechoslovakia. However, the army finally got its tanks by persuading the Germans, in 1941, to permit Scania-Vabis to build them under licence in Sweden. In all, the company produced 220 m/41s.

Scania-Vabis delivered the last of the vehicles on 11 November 1947 and the SAV took part in manoeuvres for the last time in 1968. However, an example is still on view in the Scania Museum in Södertälje.

Most of the vehicles still in service are based on the island of Gotland. A number of others are in service with the Stockholm command.

On 2 March 1943, Scania-Vabis received an order for a type of vehicle which was new to the Swedish Defence Forces—a close-support artillery vehicle consisting of a cannon mounted on a tank chassis. In the early years of the Second World War, other European forces had introduced vehicles of this type with significant success.

Two 1943 SAVs and a 1942 SKP – all faithfully restored – pictured at the Bergslag Artillery Regiment training ground in Kristinehamn.

WITH THE END OF the war, production activities at Scania-Vabis in Södertälje were once more concentrated on the civilian sector, while the end of the producer-gas era signalled the demise of the company's heavy, petrol-engined trucks. Diesel technology, which Scania-Vabis had first adopted in 1936 and undertaken in earnest with the launch of its 'unitary' engine range in 1939, had arrived to stay. A crucial factor in this development was the design, by the German company Bosch, of an injection pump which overcame the problems previously associated with the technology. The precombustion-chamber engine represented the first step in the transition and, by October 1944, a new series of twin-axle L10 diesel trucks was in production at the Södertälje plant.

The L10 was equipped with the new four-cylinder D402 engine, a 90-hp precombustion-chamber unit. The truck was equipped with a four-speed gearbox (without synchromesh) and with servo-assisted brakes. Although the new unit actually had a lower rating than its petrol-driven counterpart (the 105-hp 402), it still offered a number of advantages. The fuel was cheaper, consumption was lower (brochures published in 1944 promised 40% less than the petrol engine), engine torque was higher and the life of the unit was longer.

With a gross weight of 8.5 tonnes, the first version of the L10 was a typical all-rounder. Together with its successor, the 2L10, almost 1,300 units were built. Introduced as an 8.5-tonner in November 1946, the 2L10 was uprated to 9 tonnes with the introduction of a new front axle, new front springs and stronger auxiliary rear springs. (The growing demand for higher payloads was already beginning to make itself felt.) This model also had servo-assisted brakes and was available, from 1948 on, with an auxiliary gearbox which doubled the number of available speeds.

The L10 was the first series of Scania-Vabis trucks in which the steering wheel was on the left. In all earlier models, the wheel had been on the right—probably a hangover from the days of the horse-drawn coach, when the driver sat on that side. After the war, however, the wheel was changed to the left-hand side in compliance with international standards and in recognition of future export requirements. And there it has remained

Scania-Vabis 2L12 1946–1949

————

The first post-war series

ever since (except in models produced for export markets with left-hand traffic).

Another detail to be modified was the radiator, which was now concealed behind a protective grille. (Until then, the component had been installed unprotected at the very front of the truck, surrounded by decorative framing.) The heating, ventilation and windscreen wipers were all of improved design,

while the fuses were grouped in a special fusebox, the radiator blind was adjustable "by means of a crank from the driver's seat" and the three-man cab boasted "seat cushions and backrests of leather (as available)"!

In the haulage business, the immediate postwar years were characterised by shortages of most commodities. Although fuel again became freely available in November

With a gross weight of 8.5 tonnes and a payload of 4.3 tonnes, this Scania-Vabis 2L12 was purchased by Bollnäs Stads Byggnadskontor in January 1947. The engine was a four-cylinder precombustion-chamber diesel.

1945, and workshops and garages were swamped by vehicles requiring conversion from producer gas to liquid fuel, the national fleet still suffered from the limited availability of tyres worthy of the name. During the war, the authorities had obliged hauliers to fit sub-standard tyres or required trucks to be rebuilt to the 'p-bogie' type using car tyres. Rationing remained in force due to the con-

The D402 four-cylinder, pre-combustion-chamber diesel was part of the 'unitary' engine range developed during the early war years. However, the design became obsolescent towards the end of the decade and was superseded, in 1949, by the first Scania-Vabis direct-injection diesel.

placed with dealers Lönnbergska Motorkompaniet AB of Hudiksvall, who ordered the cabs from Nyströms in Umeå. The order was acknowledged by the sales manager of Scania-Vabis in Södertälje in Memorandum No. 5 dated 17 January 1947. The price details were as follows:

Type 2L12/D402 chassis	SKr17,650
Driver's cab	SKr1,200
2 new tyres	
Columbes 9.00/20" @	
SKr370 each:	SKr740
4 new tyres	
Firestone 8.25/20" @	
SKr323.25 each:	SKr1,293
Net invoiced price	SKr20,883

Terms of payment: Net cash on delivery

tinued scarcity of tyres after the war and the shortage was a contributory factor to the retention of the 40-kilometre range limitation. However, as part of its campaign against these restrictions, the hauliers' association itself began to import tyres and the limitation ultimately became untenable. It was finally lifted on 1 January 1947 and tyre rationing ended on 20 January, providing the long-haul industry with fresh impetus.

"Hired trucks are never available . . ."
When the finance department of the Municipality of Bollnäs met on 11 September 1947, one of the items on the agenda was a proposal to invest the sum of SKr132,195 in machinery, SKr29,700 being allocated for a truck. In § 97 of its minutes of 9 October 1947, the officers commented:

"Concerning the purchase of a truck: Until now, transport facilities for municipal works have been supplied by haulage contractors, as have street and road snow-ploughing services not furnished by the roads administration. This has provided a constant reminder of the town's need for its own truck, since hired vehicles are never available, when needed, in the same manner as would a municipal vehicle.

It is, therefore, the Department's opinion that a great deal of the transport work involved could be performed much more cheaply, particularly in view of the fact that the entire crew of the truck would be engaged in loading and unloading. For these reasons, the Department considers it appropriate that monies should be allocated for the purchase of a suitable vehicle."

The recommendation was duly adopted — and an order for no less than four trucks was

The radiator on the 2L12 was concealed behind a protective grille. On earlier models, it had been mounted unprotected at the very front, surrounded only by decorative framing.

And so it was that this Scania-Vabis 2L12, bearing chassis number 77173 and registration number X4861, came to be driven by Helge Larsson, an employee of Bollnäs Stads Byggnadskontor (the municipal engineering department). Helge was an excellent and careful driver who cared for his truck meticulously. In winter, it was used for snow-ploughing in Bollnäs and the surrounding area while, in summer, it was used to carry gravel and for general road-maintenance work.

Retired on 31 December 1958 after almost twelve years of service, and replaced by a new vehicle, the old 2L12 was acquired by Scania-Vabis dealers Bil & Buss in Bollnäs as a trade-in.

In February 1959 it was resold to Gustav Dahlgren, a Bollnäs haulier. However, it was never re-registered and was finally inherited by his sons. In 1988, Scania bought the truck from the Dahlgren brothers for restoration as part of its centenary celebrations.

SPECIFICATIONS	
Chassis	Type 2L12
Wheelbase	4.20 mm
Gross weight	8,500 kg
Engine	Type D402, precombustion-chamber diesel
Output	90 hp
Bore	115 mm
Stroke	136 mm
Swept volume	5.65 litre
No. built	1,080 (L10 series)

A Scania-Vabis LS23 was registered in Trysil, Norway in September 1948. It had been bought by the brothers Einar and Trygve Björseth, who had invested 74,300 crowns in what was one of the first large, bogie-mounted trucks in the district. Petter Hemsted, now 91, was the driver who collected the truck in Oslo.

With a gross weight of 11.4 tonnes, the truck was registered to carry 6 tonnes. First, however, it was equipped with a platform and cab by the firm of Brumunddal Mek. Verkstad og Stopperi. The cab was something special; generously sized, it could accommodate up to four people!

Petter Hemsted:

"They wanted to fit a small cab as was usual at the time, but I soon put a stop to that. A big truck should have a big cab, I said. And, that's the way it was."

The brothers Björseth used the LS23 for several years before it was acquired by hauliers Trysil Bilruter. For the next seventeen years, it was used in daily traffic around

Scania-Vabis LS23 1947–1949

The 'Trysil Jumbo'

SPECIFICATIONS	
Chassis	Type LS23
Wheelbase	5.00 m
Gross weight	11,425 kg
Engine	Type D604, 6-cyl., pre-combustion chamber diesel
Output	135 hp
Swept volume	8.47 litre
Payload	6,000 kg
No. built	280 (LS20 series)

Trysil and eastern Norway, becoming known as the 'Trysil Jumbo' or the 'ten-tonner'.

"We carried all sorts of goods over dreadful roads, in all sorts of conditions," recounts Petter Hemsted, as he renews acquaintance with 'his' truck for the first time in forty years.

The Trysil Jumbo remained in service up to 1966, by which time it had covered 600,000 kilometres.

Modifications made to the LS23 over the years included the installation of a longer platform, a cab heater and additional instrumentation.

The truck has now been restored to its original 1948 condition. Restoration was carried out under the direction of Scania Øst in Trysil, with expert assistance from the Scania Museum and other specialists.

The rejuvenated Jumbo has been selected to represent Norway among a group of veteran Scania trucks to be assembled from different export markets as part of the company's centenary celebrations.

1950–1959

Scania began to establish itself abroad and foreign operations were initiated with the opening of an engine plant in Brazil. An export department was established. No less than 43.7% of production for the decade was exported and, for the first time, more than one thousand vehicles were sold abroad in a single year (1952). Bus production reached a milestone, exceeding one thousand in 1958. Sales of VWs soared, 184,111 of the German imports being sold during the decade. And employee numbers again doubled, to approximately four thousand.

IN TECHNICAL TERMS, SCANIA-VABIS took a significant step forward when it introduced its new 40 and 60 Series trucks in 1949; the fuel consumption of the new direct-injection diesel engine was 20–25% lower compared with equivalent precombustion chamber units. Moreover, the durability of the new Scania-Vabis design was such that it soon became known as the '400,000-kilometre engine'.

The prototype had been tested two years earlier, followed shortly afterwards by practical trials in a long-duration test vehicle which ran around the clock. In January

Scania-Vabis L65
1949–1954

Scania-Vabis presents its first direct-injection diesel

1948, two engines were installed in trucks for road testing under normal traffic conditions and the unit entered production towards the end of 1949.

The new engine boasted a smaller combustion chamber than the precombustion chamber diesel. Fuel was injected directly into the cylinders through four holes in the injector, a configuration which ensured efficient combustion and improved the fuel economy dramatically.

The engine used in the 60 Series was a six-cylinder, 8.47-litre unit developing 135 hp. A four-cylinder unit (with a swept volume of

SPECIFICATIONS	
Chassis	Type L65
Wheelbase	5.00 m
Gross weight	11,000 kg
Engine	Type D622, direct-injection diesel
Output	135 hp
Bore	115 mm
Stroke	136 mm
Swept volume	8.47 litre
No. built	3,939 (L60 Series)

engine repairs—and over 1,350 presentations were made within a few years, several to trucks which had covered 600,000 kilometres without an engine overhaul.

Initially, 60-Series models were equipped with a four-speed gearbox which, in keeping with the times, was not a synchromesh unit. An auxiliary, two-speed box was available as an option, giving the driver a total of eight forward speeds.

The five-speed, synchromesh gearbox introduced by Scania-Vabis in 1951 was a first in trucks. Since first gear in the new unit was lower than that in the four-speed version, the truck was more powerful. Fifth was used as overdrive in one version, improving the fuel economy even further.

The L65 appears to have been the first truck sold by Scania-Vabis in Brazil. Although two other trucks had been shipped to the country in 1948 and 1949, the L65 was probably the first actually sold to a customer. The year was 1951.

In total, 3,939 L60 and 1,124 LS60 Series models were built.

5.65 litres and an output of 90 hp) was used in 40-Series models, while an 11.3-litre, eight-cylinder version was produced for rail buses, generator sets and marine applications.

The designers aim had been to achieve greater durability—particularly of the cylinders, piston rings and valves—in order to minimise maintenance costs. "No topping up between oil changes" promised a Scania-Vabis brochure.

Their efforts yielded results. The company soon instituted an award to any owner who drove his truck 400,000 kilometres without

This L65 was part of the first Scania-Vabis consignment shipped to Brazil in 1951. It served no less than four different owners until 1974, when it was restored as part of the Scania collection. The heavier bumper is from the 71 Series.

Decorated platform sideboards were typical of Brazilian trucks of the period.

Scania-Vabis C50 Metropol 1953

---

*Forerunner of
the modern Swedish urban bus*

"IN ALL ESSENTIAL RESPECTS, the bus is of the same design and construction as the Mack C50 tested by you eighteen months ago."

So went the introduction to a historic tender submitted by Scania-Vabis to Stockholm Tramways (later known as Stockholm Transport) on 31 May 1951, in response to an enquiry for 200 complete diesel buses for suburban routes. Awarded on 19 July, the contract not only represented the biggest order for buses in the company's history, but also signified the beginning of a new era in the field.

The Scania-Vabis Metropol was the product of a unique joint venture with the Mack Manufacturing Corporation of the USA, a project which was to be a source of mutual benefit to both companies for many years.

The project originated with a working visit to the USA by a team of Stockholm Tramways experts in 1948. One of the events arranged on that occasion was a test drive in the first of a new generation of buses built for the New York public transport system. Designed for 135 passengers (50 of whom were seated), the bus was adjudged by the Swedish visitors to be ideal for service in Stockholm. The model had wide doors to facilitate boarding and alighting, while the powerful engine (developing up to 200 hp) was used to drive a fully automatic, hydraulic gearbox. Other features included power steering and a greater than normal lock, in addition to which the heating and ventilation system was of a new design with a higher capacity.

Suitably impressed, Stockholm Tramways approached manufacturers in Sweden regarding the supply of a similar model.

As a result of this enquiry, engineers from

This Metropol covered 750,000 km in Stockholm traffic between 1953 and 1967. Renovated by Scania-Bussar, Katrineholm in 1982–83, it is now in the Scania Museum in Södertälje.

Scania-Vabis made the trip west the following year to study the American approach. Like their Stockholm Tramways counterparts, they found Mack to be the company with the highest reputation and the builder of the most reliable buses. Furthermore, Mack had now secured the New York contract, even though the rugged design of its model made it heavier than its competitors.

There was little time for action; the Stockholm Tramways' schedule was so tight that Scania-Vabis had no time to develop its own

model, prompting the idea of collaboration with Mack.

Managing Director Carl-Bertel Nathhorst travelled to the United States where, on 10 April 1949, he concluded a licence agreement giving Scania-Vabis sole manufacturing rights for the Mack C50 in Europe and sales rights throughout the world, with the exception of the USA!

A new phenomenon on the Swedish traffic scene of the early 1950s, the Scania-Vabis Metropol was to serve the people of Stock-

With a passenger capacity of 80 (48 seated and 32 standing), the Metropol was bigger than any previous Scania-Vabis bus. However, since all of its components were generously over-designed in keeping with tramway standards, it could actually accommodate up to 130.

holm until the changeover to right-hand traffic in 1967, its unique lines quickly making it a familiar sight on the streets of the city.

In several respects, the Metropol brought a new philosophy to bus traffic in Sweden. In appearance, the wide, rugged American lines made a striking impression, although the length of the vehicle made it appear unwieldy.

Drivers, however, were of a different opinion. The power steering and generous lock

enabled the huge vehicle to be manoeuvred through winding suburban streets by finger-tip control, while the hydraulic brakes also enhanced the ease of handling.

Otherwise, the American-style engine location was the most unusual feature in a Swedish bus. Installed transversely at the rear, the Scania-Vabis 11.3-litre, in-line eight was a development of the unitary engine, with direct fuel injection and a higher output of 180 hp. The power train was based on a Spicer two-stage, fully automatic, hydraulic gearbox.

Constructed on a welded sub-frame, the body was a monocoque unit on which other chassis components were mounted directly. (The Metropol was the first integrally built Swedish bus with a body of this type.) Another innovation was the fact that it was designed for one-man operation, although it carried more passengers than any previous Scania-Vabis model. This was achieved by careful control of passenger circulation, assisted by the twin entry doors ahead of the front axle and the twin exit doors midway along the side. The exit doors were opened and closed by sensors under the doorwell steps, enabling the driver to devote his full attention to embarking passengers.

Passengers found the Metropol different in a number of respects compared with earlier models. A generously-designed heating system kept the entire bus warm and cosy in winter, while the usual entry door at the rear was missing. Despite the provision of signs reading 'Entrance at front' on the side and a large sign reading 'EXIT AT REAR' behind the driver, it took time for passengers to become accustomed to the new system.

Top left: Although fingertip control was enough to steer a Metropol, the number of lock-to-lock turns was high.

Top right: The American-style transverse engine mounting was new to Sweden. The unit was easily accessible through large hatches at the rear.

The interior sound was also a unique experience. At the front, the distant whine of the engine was drowned out by the rattle of the driver's ticket machine and the click of the trip recorder (also a novel feature), while even in the bench seat at the rear, the noise was never intolerable. (This particular seat quickly became a favourite spot with youngsters. Located over the engine and offering a perfect view, it was warm and snug!)

Scania-Vabis built 200 Metropol buses, 199 for Stockholm Tramways, from 1953 to 1954. Although the model (like the Mack version on which it was based) was particularly rugged and durable, production was discontinued, mainly because the type was somewhat too large for Swedish conditions. However, the company was already working on a smaller version, the Capitol, for city traffic (see page 91).

All of the Stockholm Metropols were phased out with the changeover to right-hand traffic in 1967; although the buses were far from worn out, the cost of conversion was prohibitive.

SPECIFICATIONS	
Chassis	Type C50 Metropol
Wheelbase	6.90 m
Overall length	12.10 m
Gross weight	16,100 kg
Engine	Type D821, 8-cylinder direct-injection diesel
Output	180 hp
Swept volume	11.3 litre
Bodybuilder	Scania-Vabis
No. of passengers	48 seated, 32 standing
No. built	200

Scania-Vabis L51 Drabant 1953–1959

———

An economical workhorse

TRUCK PAYLOADS INCREASED RAPIDLY during the 1950s, rising to 5–6 tonnes as a general rule compared with 3–4 tonnes before. Meanwhile, Scania-Vabis was engaged in feverish development work to meet the growing demand for heavy trucks. With the conversion of the 'unitary' engine to direct injection in the L40/L60 Series, the company had taken a significant step forward in heavy-truck engine technology in terms of running economy, output and life. Despite this, the market was already making demands for even higher engine ratings and more innovations.

The first of the new generation of vehicles to emerge from the Södertälje plant was the L51 Drabant, which entered production in 1953. Over the following six years, production of the Drabant totalled 9,067, making it the company's volume model. Compared to its predecessor, the L40, the output of the L51's four-cylinder Scania-Vabis diesel had been increased from 90 to 100 hp, while the GVW had risen from 9.5 to between 10 and 11.5 tonnes. An all-round workhorse with a payload of 5.5 to 6.5 tonnes, the Drabant was ideal for most medium-heavy transport applications in the weight class (over 5 tonnes) which was of main interest at the time. In Sweden, the number of trucks in

this class more than quintupled between 1950 and 1961.

Technical development work at Scania-Vabis proceeded rapidly during the 1950s. Like its bigger, six-cylinder counterpart (the L71 Regent), the Drabant was equipped with a new, five-speed synchromesh gearbox with the option of an auxiliary box to double the number of speeds. Reliability and low fuel consumption were the characteristics associated with the second generation of '400,000-kilometre' engines.

Covering 400,000 kilometres without an engine overhaul was now an everyday phenomenon. Scania-Vabis promised that the Drabant "... will reduce your fuel costs. Carrying a load of 6 tonnes on the open road, the consumption will not exceed 15–17 litres per 100 kilometres. Furthermore, a Drabant will use almost no oil between changes..."

The L51 was also to make the name of Scania-Vabis known well beyond the borders of Sweden, the main export markets being the Netherlands, Norway and Belgium. The 1954 model pictured above is a Dutch-owned vehicle which is currently being renovated by its owner, Kees Zandbergen, for the Scania Museum—after 1,184,000 kilometres on the road!

SPECIFICATIONS	
Chassis	Type L51
Wheelbase	5.03 m
Gross weight	11,000 kg
Engine	Type D442
Output	100 hp
Swept volume	6.23 litre
No. built	9,067

SEVERAL MILESTONES IN TRUCK technology were reached in the 1950s. Diesel engines— now regarded as the only path to salvation at Scania-Vabis—were undergoing continuous development, while the popular L60/LS60 trucks had initiated the long-haul era. These were followed, in 1954, by the Scania-Vabis L71/LS71 (otherwise known as the Regent), a further-developed series with even more powerful engines and additional new features. The Regent was custom-built for heavy long-haul, construction-site and timber-haulage applications.

The rating of Scania's straight-six diesel

Scania-Vabis LS71 Regent 1954–1958

Custom-built for long-haul, construction-site and timber-haulage applications

was increased to 150 hp. Meanwhile, the reliability of the unit was further improved and the achievement of covering 400,000 kilometres without an engine overhaul— which attracted such attention in 1950 (see page 83)—was soon a common occurrence. Eventually, both the award and the radiator badges were withdrawn as the '400,000-kilometre engine' lost its exclusiveness and became commonplace.

Fuel consumption was reduced as direct-injection technology progressed. In advertisements, Scania-Vabis promised "minimal fuel consumption" for the L71, adding that

The grille on our featured vehicle proudly bears a '40,000-mil engine' badge, a distinction which was awarded when the straight-six diesel had covered this distance without an engine overhaul. (The 'mil' is a commonly used Swedish unit equal to 10 kilometres.) However, this mark of reliability—which aroused great interest when it was introduced in 1950—was now commonplace.

Bought by hauliers Kallebäcks Transport AB of Gothenburg in 1957, this LS71 served the Gothenburg-Norrköping and Gothenburg-Malmö long-haul routes for twenty years, pulling a two-axle or three-axle trailer. Later, it was used locally as a tractor unit. By the time it was retired in 1980, it had almost 1.5 million kilometres on the clock. The wheelbase was shortened and, following an accident, the original cab was replaced by a more modern steel type.

steering and air brakes on the 71 Series. The Regent was available with air brakes as an option from the commencement of production in 1954 and was equipped with power steering in 1955. Combined with air brakes, power steering greatly eased the work of the driver and improved the standard of safety significantly. Drivers were loud in their praise of the feature, particularly when it came to reversing fully-loaded rigs, an operation which had hitherto called for tough arm muscles.

With the growing popularity of truck-mounted ancillaries such as cranes, hoists and tippers, simple means of using the engine to power such equipment were required. The new gearbox was equipped with a 25-hp power take-off for this purpose.

Brochures published in 1954 proclaimed that the Regent was available in three colours, "Scania grey, light grey and dark green, with red, blue and cream-coloured radiator decor". The day of the exclusive finish was still some years off!

In all, over 7,700 L71s and LS71s were built between 1954 and 1958, by which time the next stage of development was imminent.

topping up the oil between normal changes would be unnecessary.

The five-speed synchromesh gearbox (now standard) was available, from the outset, with the option of an auxiliary gearbox which doubled the number of speeds and provided 45% more traction in bottom gear—a feature which quickly became popular for hauling the heaviest of loads, particularly in the forests of northern Sweden. From October 1956 on, this model was also available with a new design of rear axle with a heavy-duty double reduction.

Other Scania-Vabis 'firsts' included power

SPECIFICATIONS	
Chassis	Type LS71
Wheelbase	5.00 m
Gross weight	17,000 kg
Engine	Type D642, 6-cylinder direct-injection diesel
Output	150 hp
Bore	115 mm
Stroke	150 mm
Swept volume	9.35 litre
No. built	2,231

ed favourable load distribution and, when the axle weight was utilised to the full—as in the BF71 which succeeded the BF60—the model took up to 35% more passengers than any other Swedish bus of the time.

However, the BF remained a 'mere' B model with a relocated engine. Realising that the design could be improved even further, the company's engineers commenced work on a 'pure' BF model in 1954. This was introduced in 1956 under the designation BF73, the figures indicating that it was an 'intermediate' model pending the availability of the D10 engine, which appeared in the 75 Series in 1959. The BF73 boasted several innovations which paved the way for Scania-Vabis's later front-engined chassis.

The frame was further refined. A low-slung type (not, in itself, a particularly novel feature), it was also equipped with factory-fitted 'outriggers' in the form of crossmember extensions which projected beyond the side members. Whereas, previously, bodybuilders had fitted their own crossmembers on top of the frame to support the body, the body floor could now be mounted directly on the frame. In addition, the chassis was 'tidied' to accommodate as many types of body as possible.

The BF73 was Scania-Vabis's first front-engined bus with power steering—a necessary feature given the high front-axle weight. A generous wheel lock, air brakes and a synchromesh gearbox made the model safe and easy to drive, offering drivers some compensation for doubling as conductors.

The BF73 soon accounted for the greater proportion of sales of front-engined buses. In Sweden, it was purchased by operators including Swedish Railways (SJ) and the Björknäs company, one of whose models (with a light-alloy body) is pictured above.

INTRODUCED IN 1949, THE first BF model signalled the start of a new trend—one-man-operated buses. On the BF60 (the first model), the engine was relocated ahead of the front axle, creating enough front overhang to provide space for an entry door.

The demand came from several quarters, including the Björknäs bus company. However, interest from Scania-Vabis was lukewarm until the Dutch importer, Beers, used a converted Scania-Vabis bus to show that the concept was actually fairly simple.

One-man buses quickly became standard on city and suburban services, and the BF models were appreciated for their high passenger capacity. The relocated engine afford-

Scania-Vabis BF73 1956–1959

First front-engined bus with power steering

SPECIFICATIONS	
Chassis	Type BF73
Wheelbase	5.75 m
Gross weight	14,500 kg
Engine	Type D635, 6-cylinder, direct-injection diesel
Output	150 hp
Swept volume	9.35 litre
Bodybuilder	Svenska Karosseri Verkstäderna
No. of passengers	40 seated, 6 standing
No. built	483

DESPITE WHAT WAS SAID about the manoeuvrability of the Scania-Vabis Metropol, the design was best suited to wide, straight American boulevards and to Swedish suburbs. In the city, it was too big—at least in the opinion of the Stockholm authorities, who considered that the high axle weight was damaging the city's streets and bridges.

Thus, it came as no surprise when Stockholm Tramways (SS) made an enquiry for a new, smaller city bus the very year (1953) in which production of the Metropol commenced. The axle weight was not to exceed 8 tonnes, while the maximum permissible gross weight was to be 14 tonnes.

Scania-Vabis submitted a design proposal for a shortened version of the Metropol with a six-cylinder engine, as well as a lighter variant equipped with somewhat lighter axles. Initial deliveries were promised ten months following receipt of order!

In September 1954, SS ordered a series of 180 buses of the lighter type. This model was designated the Scania-Vabis C70 Capitol.

The Capitol was subsequently refined in several stages, with minor modifications to the exterior. The C75—a version which was equipped with air suspension all round as an alternative to the leaf-spring type and was powered by the new Scania-Vabis six-cylinder D10 engine—appeared in 1959. Air suspension was revolutionary, not only in terms of riding comfort; chassis components and

Scania-Vabis Capitol 1955–1964

A shortened 'Swedish' version of the Metropol city bus

body also benefited from the gentler ride. This was later utilised to achieve a substantial reduction in weight.

The next stage, represented by the C76—a model with air suspension as standard equipment and the more powerful D11 engine—was introduced in 1963.

In all, 429 Capitols were built. Most of the original models remained in service in Swedish towns and cities until the changeover to right-hand traffic in 1967, when they became redundant (some being shipped to Pakistan as part of an aid programme). Of the later models, many were rebuilt for right-hand traffic and remained in service until the early 1980s. Only a few bodied Capitols were exported. Between 1959 and 1965, however, 135 chassis were shipped to Argentina, where they were coachworked for service as long-distance buses.

SPECIFICATIONS	
Chassis	Type C75
Wheelbase	6.12 m
Overall length	10.48 m
Gross weight	15,000 kg
Engine	D10, 6-cylinder direct-injection diesel
Output	165 hp
Swept volume	10.26 litre
Gearbox	Fully automatic, 3-speed hydraulic
Bodybuilder	Scania-Vabis
No. of passengers	34 seated, 32 standing
No. built	120 (429)

WHEN SCANIA-VABIS STARTED to sell the 75 Series in May 1958, it little suspected that the model would become the longest-lived ever. Renamed in succession the 76, 110 and 111, it became more comfortable, more powerful and heavier (although little changed in appearance) over the years, and remained in production until August 1980.

The truck was built initially in a twin-axle version (L75) and a three-axle version with an auxiliary axle (LS75). From August 1958 on, it was also available as a three-axle version with a double-drive bogie (LT75). Gross

Scania-Vabis
LT75
1958–1963

———

Manufactured for 22 years, continuously improved and renamed three times

weights ranged from 12.6 to 22.0 tonnes. The basic gearbox offered five speeds, or ten with the addition of an optional auxiliary box.

The new model was a modern heavy truck which met the demands of the postwar market, especially in terms of engine rating and comfort. It was powered by a new, direct-injection, six-cylinder diesel developing 165 hp and, from February 1961 onwards, by Scania-Vabis's first turbocharged truck engine with an output of 205 hp.

Although the customer was free to specify any make of cab, most of the units were sup-

Hauri Kiesgruben & Transport AG of Seon bought this Scania-Vabis LT75 in 1962. Equipped with a tipper body by Wirz, the truck became the first Scania-Vabis three-axle tipper in Switzerland. It was used for tough motorway construction work in which axle weight limits did not apply. After ten years, the bogie weight was increased to twenty tonnes, enabling the LT75 to be driven on the road. The truck ended its career in the company's quarry in Seon.

headlamps (a novel feature) were the work of designer Björn Karlström.

The driver's station was unique in that, for the first time in a Scania-Vabis truck, the instruments were grouped in front of the driver rather than in the centre of the dashboard. The earlier type of brake pedal, which required a high leg action, was replaced by one at the same level as the accelerator, making operation of the air brakes more comfortable for the driver.

Unveiled in January 1963, the succeeding 76 Series was produced for five years, during which several new features were introduced. The standard and turbocharged engines were uprated to 190 and 260 hp respectively, while the GVWs were also increased and the braking system was split into two circuits for enhanced safety. Furthermore, since the parking brake was equipped with a pneumatic servo, it functioned as a third, emergency braking circuit. Power steering became standard in 1967.

A major technical innovation introduced in 1964 was the combination of the main and auxiliary gearboxes, creating a ten-speed unit which was 50 kg lighter and occupied less space than the original 'five-plus-two' configuration.

Scania-Vabis's own cab was introduced in 1966. Although very similar to the Be-Ge version, the new unit was made entirely of steel. The cab used was that from the L36—a 'normal' cab which was now also available in lengthened rest cab and sleeper versions. The transition between cab and bonnet was now smoother—one of the very few external modifications made to the truck in twenty-two years.

Scania-Vabis built over 38,600 of the 75 and 76 Series—a total which, with the 110 and 111, was to be trebled before this enduring design was finally discontinued.

plied by AB Be-Ge Karosserifabrik of Oskarshamn. The cab was then installed by Scania-Vabis as a factory-fitted extra.

As a European 'first', the cab, bonnet and wings were built as an integral unit which was supported on rubber mountings, offering improved insulation against both noise and vibration. However, the construction called for a new design of bonnet to replace the butterfly-wing type. The solution was the 'alligator' bonnet which opened straight upwards like the jaws of that ferocious beast.

The bonnet and wings, with their recessed

Hauri did not retire its LT75 from service until 1989, when it was restored to its original condition by Scania dealers Hächler AG of Othmarsingen. The truck is now in the Scania Museum.

SPECIFICATIONS	
Chassis	Type LT75
Wheelbase	3.80 m
Gross weight	22,000 kg
Engine	Type DS10 (D10)
Output	205 hp (165 hp)
Bore	127 mm
Stroke	135 mm
Swept volume	10.3 litre
No. built	310

1960–1969

International expansion continued. In 1964, a major assembly plant was opened at Zwolle in the Netherlands. In that year, Scania-Vabis's invoiced sales exceeded SKr1 billion for the first time and over 60% of production was exported. Other milestones included the production of 10,000 vehicles in 1965, while the workforce exceeded 10,000 and the 100,000th truck was delivered in 1966. The company commenced production of its own cabs at Oskarshamn and busbuilding was transferred to Katrineholm. The 'Program Scania' range was launched and the decade ended with the merger with Saab to form Saab-Scania.

Scania-Vabis
LB76
1963–68

*The first modern, forward-control
truck for international traffic*

THE NEED FOR RESTRICTIONS of various types first became apparent with the growth of European truck traffic in the 1960s. In most European countries, vehicle lengths were limited to 15 metres for semi-trailer rigs and 18 metres for truck and trailer combinations, while a series of other measures was introduced to encourage rail freight. However, the march of progress could not be denied, and trucks became both more numerous and more powerful. Engine power became a selling feature, while safety standards improved.

Powered by a bigger and more powerful straight six-cylinder engine, the Scania-Vabis 76 Series was introduced in 1963 – and, for the first time in thirty years, a forward-control truck of the 'bulldog' type (the LB76) was being built at Södertälje. The length restrictions in force in the company's increasingly important export markets provided the main incentive for the development of short cabs. Although the debate regarding overall lengths was gathering momentum in Sweden, it was not until 1966 that a train length limitation (a generous 24 metres) was imposed.

Strength requirements were, however, imposed on truck cabs in Sweden in the early 1960s and, although the Swedish steel cabs

The right-hand drive version of the LB76 arrived in Britain in 1966. The 'bulldog' shape was necessitated by strict length restrictions. Now with about 1.3 million miles on the clock, the first of these models to be sold in the country is lovingly cared for by Ray Hingley in West Bromwich. (The truck is dubbed the 'Swedish Ancestor'.)

The 1966 LB76 Super boasted a DS11 direct-injected, turbocharged diesel developing 220 hp, a ten-speed gearbox, power steering, dual-circuit air brakes and a gross weight of 16.5 tonnes. A total of 4,693 LB76/LBS76 models was built between January 1963 and February 1968.

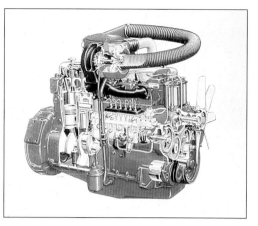

The spring brake chamber-type of parking brake developed in the USA was introduced later, the handbrake lever and pneumatic brake servo being replaced by a small panel-mounted lever which operated the brake by means of a pneumatic valve.

Like the bonneted L76, the LB76 was available in both twin-axle and three-axle versions with gross weights of 16.5 and 21 (later 22) tonnes respectively. The engine was soon uprated – to 240 hp in 1964 and to 260 hp three years later – as the engineers worked incessantly to meet the demand for higher outputs, making increasing use of turbocharging (a method of extracting higher power from the same cubic capacity) for this purpose. Although the technique was still regarded with a degree of scepticism by most of the company's European competitors, developments were to show that Scania-Vabis had chosen the correct option – and the feature is now commonplace.

Continuing in production until February 1968, the LB76 heralded the boom in forward-control trucks.

of the day easily complied with the standards, certain malicious European tongues were spreading the word that protectionist Sweden was using the measure as a pretext to protect its truck industry. Whatever the facts, Swedish safety cabs were used as an advertising feature, making a contribution to the growing success of Scania-Vabis in export markets.

The driver who could crawl, in one piece, from his crumpled but intact cab after a severe accident, could thank the designers for his survival. Other safety innovations in the 76 Series included dual-circuit brakes and power steering.

In 1964, Scania-Vabis took a significant step into Europe when it commenced assembly of the 76 Series at Zwolle in the Netherlands. Two years later, the right-hand drive version became the first of a series of successful export models to conquer Britain (where the very first LB76 to be imported is still going strong).

Nicknamed the 'Summer Scania' by Swedish drivers, the model also became popular in Sweden, despite the necessity of opening the front hatch in hot weather. What driver can forget the ten-speed box with its twin gear levers, which called for a highly skilled gear-changing technique? Or the handbrake with its air gauge? Other standard features included differential locking, air brakes and a synchromesh gearbox.

Above: With its short cab, the LB76 was designed to comply with international demands for maximum cargo space within a limited overall length.

Top right: The DS11 direct-injection turbo developed 220 hp. The rating was later increased to 240 and then to 260 hp.

The maintenance-free, centrifugal oil filter was a patented Scania-Vabis feature.

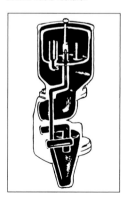

SPECIFICATIONS	
Chassis	Type LB76
Wheelbase	3.00 m
Gross weights	GVW 16,250 kg; GCW 32,500 kg
Engine	Type DS11 (D11) 6-cyl. direct-injection diesel
Output	240 hp (190 hp)
Bore	127 m
Stroke	145 mm
Swept volume	11.0 litre
No. built	2,575

Scania-Vabis CF buses 1959–66

The first integrally-built front-engined bus

WITH FIVE YEARS EXPERIENCE of integral construction and armed with its successful BF73 chassis (dating from 1956), Scania-Vabis introduced the first integrally-built bus of its own design (the CF75) in 1959. (The model was also produced as the CF65 with lighter axles.) The introduction coincided with the launch of the new truck and bus diesel engines with designations ending in '5'.

In all essential respects, the CF65/75 chassis was based on the BF73 (or BF65/75 as it was now known). However, the frame was lower and considerably lighter since it was welded to the body frame to create a monocoque construction. The outer panels were of aluminium or, in the case of complicated shapes, of glass fibre-reinforced plastic.

Despite its size (the overall length was up to 12.2 metres), the kerb weight of the bus was considerably less than 9 tonnes. Since it was also relatively low (2.9 metres), its size was not obvious from the front. However, the impression was different when the vehicle was viewed rounding a corner with the large sweep of the 3.5-metre rear overhang. The interior was bright and airy thanks to the large glass surfaces and grey-white 'hospital-

type' plastic panels on the walls.

The bus was equipped with a front door for tourist use, and two or three doors for city operation. In the latter case, the rear door was intended for passenger entry with a conductor on board. Pneumatic rear suspension was available as the latest innovation.

With the introduction of the 11-litre engine in 1963, the designations were changed to CF66 and CF76. Production ceased in 1966 when plant capacity was required to build the new CR76 city bus.

Some of the 912 CF buses built are still in service today, many with hundreds of thousands of kilometres on the clock and attractively fitted out as holiday campers.

Exports of the CF models were limited to the lone example (illustrated above) shipped to Iceland. The interior was bright and airy due to the large windows and the grey-white wall panels.

SPECIFICATIONS	
Chassis	Scania-Vabis CF65
Wheelbase	6.12 m
Gross weight	14,300 kg
Engine	Type D10, 6-cylinder direct-injection diesel
Output	165 hp
Swept volume	10.26 litre
Body by	Scania-Vabis
No. of passengers	50 seated, 25 standing
No. built	496 (910)

WORK ON A NEW generation of integrally-built rear-engined buses to replace the Capitol models was commenced in 1962. At this time, the Swedish parliament had not yet taken a decision in principle to implement the changeover to right-hand traffic. However, the Swedish Local Transport Association had unveiled its 'standard bus' concept – essentially a specification for a comfortable, passenger-friendly urban bus – and, since the ideas which it embodied were adjudged to be sound and realistic, it was used as the basis for the new Scania-Vabis CR76.

Scania-Vabis CR76 1966–1971

A new standard for buses

Two features received high priority – low weight and a low floor. To lower the floor level, it was obvious that the engine would have to be located at the rear. As in the last of the Capitols (the C76), the unit chosen was the normally-aspirated, 190-hp D11 which gave the lighter CR76 impressive performance.

Awakening environmental consciousness also made a contribution. The engine was tuned for minimum smoke emission, a problem which the designers of the Capitol had attempted to solve using an air injector in the exhaust pipe. In addition, the engine

The low floor, wide double doors at the front and middle, and a bright interior were familiar features of the CR76. The extremely low floor level was made possible by the monocoque construction without side members.

pared with the Capitol, the floor level was lowered by 20 cm to 64 cm (extremely low by the standards of the day), greatly facilitating passenger boarding.

The final stages of development were attended by great urgency. Production of the CR76 commenced only about a year before Sweden made the change to right-hand traffic – and operators were obviously anxious to have their new vehicles in time.

To deal with the situation, Scania-Vabis greatly increased its output of buses, tripling the rate of production from the Södertälje plant. In the first year, almost 500 CR76s were delivered to twenty-five Swedish towns and cities and a limited number were exported to other Scandinavian countries.

Now a reality, the 'standard bus' was to become popular with drivers and passenger alike. Together with its renamed successor, the CR110, the CR76 remained in production until 1971, when the truly silent city bus appeared on the scene.

compartment was sealed, the design of the silencer was improved and a thermostatically controlled radiator fan was installed to reduce the external noise level.

Radical new approaches were adopted in designing the body – a monocoque type which also incorporated the light-alloy outer panels. Even the steel anti-collision members around the body had a load-bearing function, while the bulky side members were dispensed with.

The advantages of the new body design were exploited to the full in the CR76. Com-

The Malmö Tramway Company (MSS) was first to buy the CR76, ordering a total of 130. The last of these was used in service until 1989. In that year, Malmö Transport (successors to MSS) completed a fine restoration job on the CR76 featured here.

SPECIFICATIONS	
Chassis	Scania-Vabis CR76
Wheelbase	5.90 m
Overall length	11.47 m
Gross weight	15,500 kg
Engine	Scania-Vabis D11, 6-cylinder, direct-injection diesel
Output	190 hp
Swept volume	11.0 litre
Gearbox	Fully-automatic, 2-stage, ZF Hydromedia 2 HP 45
Bodybuilder	Scania-Vabis
No. of passengers	80 (32 seated)
No. built	1,012

Scania L50
1968–1975

The smallest truck in the new 'Program Scania' range introduced in 1968

THE L50 MAY WELL prove to be the last 'light' truck produced by Scania (always allowing for future developments). This 12-tonne truck was the smallest in the new range launched by the company in February 1968, when it was introduced along with the larger 80 and 110 models.

Not entirely new, the L50 was, in fact, an improved version of the L36—a model introduced in autumn 1964. However, the truck was now equipped with a new design of front axle and was also fitted, in June 1971, with spring brake chambers—a new (and welcome) feature of the Scania range. Instead of the traditional handbrake lever, the parking brake in the 'new' model was applied by means of a small lever on the instrument panel.

The light, four-cylinder, 5.2-litre, 95-hp diesel was retained in the L50, the rating being increased to 105 hp in April 1970. In addition, the DS5—a turbocharged, 120-hp unit—was available as an option to owners who required even higher power.

Scania departed from its principles in one respect; the gearbox was a German unit. By 1971, however, the L50 was equipped with a Scania gearbox designed specifically for the model. On the other hand, the original two-speed final drive was of the company's own design. Giving the driver a total of ten speeds, this was standard equipment on L50s built for gravel haulage, and for quarry and construction-site work.

The two alternative wheelbases of the L36 chassis were complemented by a third of 5.40 metres, providing a platform length of 6 metres and making the truck suitable for carrying palletised loads.

As the very first cab of Scania's own design

Owned by the Krarup dairy cooperative in Denmark, the milk truck pictured here bore the designation Scania 50 Super. And a super truck it proved to be! Every day for fifteen years, it made four milk collections from the farmers in and around the little village on the island of Funen. The total quantity of milk which it carried (7,000 litres on each trip) is impossible to estimate. Edvard Knutsen (its driver throughout this entire period) notes that the truck covered 469,000 kilometres. Although this may not seem extraordinary for fifteen years of service, it should be remembered that the farms in the area are close together!

and construction, the all-steel unit, introduced on the L35, was also used on the L50.

Cab safety test regulations, including impact testing with a one-tonne pendulum weight, were introduced in Sweden in 1961. The tests were carried out first by Scania and then by the National Testing Institute for Agricultural Machinery at Alnarp, near Uppsala. Always mindful of the consequences of failure with production already under way, Scania engineers invariably found the occasion a test of nerves over the years.

The Scania L50 became popular as a delivery truck and was produced in many different versions for special applications. Many readers will undoubtedly remember the snub-nosed model, while drivers will certainly remember the bulge in the floor created by the left-hand front-wheel housing.

The model was discontinued in 1975 after 4,183 had been built. No less than 2,578 of these were exported, the majority to neighbouring Scandinavian countries.

The attractive blue and white L50 with its 7,000-litre tank served the Krarup cooperative for fifteen years. Retired just before the creamery's centenary in 1987, it was replaced immediately by two new Scanias—an 82M and a 92M, both with 9,000-litre capacities.

SPECIFICATIONS	
Chassis	Type L50
Wheelbase	4.20 m
Gross weight	12,000 kg
Engine	Type DS5 (D5) 4-cylinder, direct-injection, supercharged diesel
Output	120 hp (95–105 hp)
Bore	115 mm
Stroke	125 mm
Swept volume	5.2 litre
No. built	4,183

IN JUNE 1969, SCANIA-VABIS began to manufacture a direct-injection, turbocharged V8 engine for its new LB, LBS and LBT140 Super trucks. Boasting an impressive 350-hp rating, the new power unit immediately gave Scania the lead in the race for higher outputs in which European truckmakers were then engaged, and represented a significant increase over the 260-hp rating of the straight 6-cylinder, 11-litre unit. While the demand for higher outputs was encouraged by the higher gross weights and axle weights permitted by advances in road development, international sources were also calling for trucks to adapt more efficiently to traffic rhythms, requiring improved performance in terms of speed and acceleration.

West Germany had declared its intention of introducing a minimum rating of 8 hp per tonne gross weight (equivalent to a 304-hp engine in a 38-tonne rig) in 1972—a major

Scania-Vabis LBS140 1969–1976

The most power-ful standard truck in Europe, powered by a 350-hp V8 engine

step at a time when many international hauliers were trundling along with a mere 200 hp or so under the bonnet. As a result, the new Scania-Vabis engine attracted justifiable international attention when it was unveiled at the Frankfurt International Motor Show in September 1969.

The company had, for several years, been testing a V8 design as the most suitable type for the even higher powers which would be required in the future. The 14-litre capacity offered major potential for continued development, while the V8 configuration created a compact unit which did not occupy too much space under the forward-control cab. Turbocharging—which Scania had developed in the 1950s, decades before it was adopted by carmakers—now became standard. With a maximum speed of 2,300 r/min, the first generation of Scania V8s delivered a maximum torque of 1,225 Nm at 1,400 r/min.

A new design of turbocompressor was used to supply both banks of cylinders. Five-hole injectors were introduced for more efficient mixing of the fuel and air while, for the first time, the injection pump was equipped with a built-in smoke limiter. Other technical advances included gear-driven auxiliaries (lubricating oil pump, brake compressor, coolant pump, injection pump and power-steering pump).

The LB140 was equipped with the same new, forward-control, tilting cab which had been introduced one and a half years earlier (in February 1968) in the LB110 (see page 106). Lionel Sherrow, the Englishman who designed the cab, created a completely new Scania-Vabis image while greatly improving the standard of in-cab comfort. Features such as the ease of entry, the elegant driving environment and the generously designed fresh-air system were all praised, while ser-

Purchased in 1972, this LBS140 is still operated by KGT Trafik AB of Kristianstad, Sweden. After covering 2,900,000 kilometres in long-haul service between Kristianstad and Stockholm and, later, between Kristianstad and Skövde, with hauliers ASG, it was used on the Kristianstad-Malmö run from 1987 to 1989.

vice was greatly facilitated by the tilting cab. Air conditioning became available at a later date.

Popular with drivers, the LB110 and LB140 made a significant contribution to Scania-Vabis's success in export markets in the late 1960s and early 1970s.

SPECIFICATIONS	
Chassis	Type LBS140
Wheelbase	4.60 m
Gross weight	22,500 kg
Engine	Type DS14, V8, direct-injection, turbocharged diesel
Output	350 hp
Bore	127 mm
Stroke	140 mm
Swept volume	14.2 litre
No. built	5,132

THE FORWARD-CONTROL CAB on the Scania-Vabis LB76 quickly became outdated; the continental market was now demanding that cabs of this type should afford easier entry and improved access for engine service. These requirements were met by relocating the step ahead of the front wheel and designing the cab to tilt. Equipped with these features, the LB110 superseded the LB76 in February 1968.

Scania was widely praised for the LB110 cab, which was designed by Englishman Lionel Sherrow. Easy to enter, the elegant interior offered the driver a high standard of comfort. The trade press was loud in its praise of the workplace which Scania had created for drivers, while buyers had a choice of a standard cab or sleeper.

Power steering, air brakes and a servo-assisted clutch made the driver's work much easier, while the generously dimensioned fresh-air system was much appreciated on hot summer days. An air-conditioned cab, with the unit installed in the roof-hatch opening, became available later.

The cab was designed for fast and practical service. A large front hatch provided access to the dipsticks for the engine oil and power-steering fluid, to the filler caps for the oil,

Scania LB110 1968–1974

Equipped with a tilting cab for ease of service

SPECIFICATIONS	
Chassis	Type LB110
Wheelbase	5.00 m
Gross weight	16,000 kg
Engine	Type DS11 (D11)
Output	260 (190) hp
Swept volume	11.0 litre
No. built	14,338

power-steering fluid and clutch-servo fluid, to the brake system antifreeze reservoir and to the cold-starting controls.

The complete cab tilted forward for major service work. Performed by a single person with the aid of a manually operated hydraulic system, the operation took about a minute. As a safety measure, pumping was also required to return the cab to the normal position, ensuring that it was locked in all positions by the hydraulics.

The Scania LB110 was equipped with a ten-speed gearbox as standard equipment. The main five-speed unit was supplemented by a planetary-type range gearbox which doubled the number of speeds available to the driver. (In spite this, one of the journalists who test-drove the truck was of the opinion that the high 4th and low 5th positions were so close in terms of reduction ratio that they did not represent a useful interval.)

Buyers had the choice of two engines—the 190-hp D11 and the 260-hp, turbocharged DS11—both six-cylinder units. Over 14,000 LB110s were built up to September 1974.

Photographed in Lindau, the model featured below is a German-registered LB110 Super.

S<small>CANIA CALLED IT THE</small> LA82. To the Swedish Defence Forces, it was the Ltgb 957. But to the troops, the truck has always been known as the 'Anteater'—the nickname it acquired because of its long, sloping front end.

A new design in almost every detail, the first Anteater was supplied to the military in 1960. With a kerb weight of almost 11 tonnes, it was one of the biggest trucks ever built in Sweden. Operating in difficult terrain, it could carry 5 tonnes on the platform while towing a heavy artillery piece weighing 10 tonnes.

In the prototypes, the unmistakable bonnet concealed an eight-in-line engine, while the 440 production models delivered by 1962 were equipped with a 220-hp, six-cylinder unit. All six wheels of the three-axle vehicle were driving wheels.

The differential locks, 10-tonne towing winch, power steering, pneumatic clutch servo and ten-speed gearbox were all features which contributed to the excellent terrain mobility of the vehicle.

Scania-Vabis LA82 1960–1962

What is the true life of an 'Anteater'?

SPECIFICATIONS	
Chassis	Type LA82
Wheelbase	3.40 + 1.32 m
Gross weight	16,000 kg
Engine	Type DS10
Output	220 hp
Swept volume	10.3 litre
No. built	440

On the road, the Anteater had a top speed of 75 km/h with 8 tonnes on the platform and 20 tonnes behind. The front end of the platform was designed to accommodate a personnel cabin (for example, to house the artillery crew), while a machine gun was mounted on top of the driver's cab.

So, what is the true life of an Anteater? As though to answer this question, the Swedish army overhauled and rebuilt 300 of its best-maintained units between 1983 and 1987, equipping them for service as cross-country bridge-laying vehicles until at least 2005.

In its new role, the model will be employed by the engineering corps to transport and lay down the structural elements of pontoon bridges, using a special-purpose loader to place each new section in the water as the floating structure is built.

As a result of this development, the L82 Anteater has been assigned yet another succinct military designation—Brotgb 9572A MT.

1970–1979

A decade of growth, with production showing a twofold and exports a threefold increase. Exports totalled 83% of production, exceeding 10,000 for the first time in 1970 and 20,000 in 1979. A new plant was opened at Tucuman in Argentina.
Milestones:
1974 – over 5,000 separate engines
1978 – over 2,000 buses
1979 – more than 20,000 employees
1979 – profits reach SKr1 billion
Scania Division began to manufacture petrol engines and gearboxes for Saab cars.

Scania SBA111/SBAT111
1975–1990

*Defence Forces demand high
mobility and fast service of new
cross-country vehicle*

Iɴ 1964, Sᴄᴀɴɪᴀ-Vᴀʙɪs and FMV (the Swedish Defence Matériel Administration) held initial discussions regarding the supply of a new cross-country vehicle. An order was placed in 1969 and the first of two prototypes, known as the Scania LBA110 and Scania LBAT110, were delivered a year and a half later.

After testing under summer and winter conditions, in wet and cold test chambers, and over the most difficult terrain imaginable—and after yet another series of prototypes had been produced—deliveries to the Defence Forces commenced just before Christmas 1975. By this time, the trucks were known as the SBA111 and SBAT111.

Scania's contract with the military was unique. The price of the new vehicles was to be determined by their operating and maintenance costs. If maintenance costs were low, the Defence Department was to pay a higher price per truck—and vice versa. Not surprisingly, the test programme was intensive.

The vehicles are built to operate in extremely difficult terrain, with the capability of negotiating a 6-in-10 climb and operating fully-loaded on a 4-in-10 side slope. With a ground clearance of 40 cm, they are designed to clear diagonal obstructions, rocks and similar obstacles 60 cm high with all wheels in contact with the ground.

Comfort and simplicity of service were major priorities. Well insulated and equipped with comfortable seats, the forward-control cab tilts forwards to afford easy access to the engine, while the engine itself is designed for replacement in the field—in a mere four hours!

Built to operate in extremely difficult terrain, the SBA/SBAT111 is designed to negotiate a 6-in-10 climb and operate fully-loaded on a 4-in-10 side slope. The model shown is an SBAT111.

The automatic gearbox—a six-speed unit which enables the vehicle to be driven at speeds from 3 to 80 km/h—was another of the specified requirements. A special foot control facilitates brake operation, permitting high-precision driving in particularly difficult areas of terrain.

The trucks are produced in two versions. Powered by the Scania six-cylinder, 220-hp D11 diesel engine, the twin-axle SBA111 has a load capacity of 4.5 tonnes and is capable of hauling a 6-tonne trailer across country.

The three-axle SBAT111 is equipped with the supercharged, 300-hp DS11 engine, and is capable of carrying 6 tonnes on the platform while hauling a 12-tonne trailer. All axles are driven in both models.

Scania's design philosophy was to use as many identical components as possible to maximise interchangeability between the vehicles. The axles are a typical example.

The Defence Forces specifications called for special-purpose designs. As an example, a special method of attachment has been devised to ensure that the platform remains level at all times, despite the often severe torsion of the frame in rugged country. In

Top left: The Swedish Air Force SBAT111 emergency vehicle is operated by one man and has a GVW of 16 tonnes. The fire pump capacity is 2,500 l/min.

Top right: Under ordinary driving conditions, the SBA111 snow slinger can reach 70 km/h. In operation, the vehicle 'reverses' at up to 20 km/h.

addition, the engines are equipped with oil pumps designed to operate at steep angles, while the starting equipment is designed to operate even in -40°C arctic cold.

The vehicles are used primarily to transport artillery and personnel, the troops being housed in a covered, heated cabin on the platform, while the gun is towed behind.

To date, a total of 2,700 SBA111/SBAT111s have been delivered to the Swedish Defence Forces, who expect the vehicles to remain in service until 2020! A further 700 have been exported, while a number of special versions have also been built.

Between 1977 and 1979, the Royal Swedish Air Force acquired 80 SBA111s as snow-clearing vehicles. In this application, the truck is 'reversed' from an auxiliary cab installed back-to-back with the normal cab. The snow-slinger engine is a Scania DS14.

The Royal Swedish Air Force has also purchased an SBAT111 as an emergency vehicle. Among other equipment, the truck is fitted with a foam cannon capable of extinguishing fires at a range of 45 metres. Scania cross-country vehicles are also used as radar trucks and crane trucks—and even as 'ordinary' passenger buses in Iceland.

An SBA111 cross-country chassis with a purpose-built body is the ideal tourist bus for expeditions to the interior of Iceland. The vehicle can negotiate glacial streams and the hilly, almost roadless, pumice stone-covered terrain without undue difficulty.

SPECIFICATIONS		
Chassis	Type SBA111	SBAT111
Wheelbase	4.00 m	3.55 + 1.48 m
Gross weight	13,400 kg	16,600 kg
Engine	Type D11	DS11
Output	220 hp	300 hp
Bore	127 mm	127mm
Stroke	145 mm	145 mm
Swept volume	11.0 litre	11.0 litre
No. built	1,803 (SBA111);	1,608 (SBAT111)

Scania L111
1974–1982

*The last version
of Scania's
highest-volume
model*

THE APPEARANCE OF THE L111 in September 1974 signified the final chapter in an era which spanned more than two decades. Although many technical advances had been made since the introduction of the L75 (see page 92) in 1958, the two models were almost identical in appearance.

The L75 was succeeded, first by the L76, then by the L110 in 1968. Whereas the same engine was used in the latter two models, a major technical innovation in the form of a ten-speed, range-type gearbox was introduced in July 1971. The new unit simplified the task of selecting the ten speeds available with the five gear-lever positions.

A year before the L110 was renamed the L111, the cab interior was modified to create a more congenial driving environment. Headlamp washers were also provided.

The parking brake provides an excellent example of how this enduring model developed over the years. In the earlier models, the brake consisted of a mechanical linkage operated by a floor-mounted lever, which the driver was obliged to operate several times when parking (the type being known as the mechanical multi-pull brake). However, the L76 was equipped with a single-pull brake with a pneumatic servo, while the L110

SPECIFICATIONS	
Chassis	Type L111
Wheelbase	3.80 m
Gross weight	(with semi-trailer) 40,000 kg
Engine	DS11 (D11)
Output	296 (203) hp
Swept volume	11.0 litre
No. built	30,150

boasted the spring brake chamber-type used on modern trucks. In the latter case, light movement of a small lever on the instrument panel is sufficient to apply the brake.

The L111 was available with more powerful engines with outputs of 203 and 296 hp. In May 1977, customers were also offered the option of a 305-hp unit. Meanwhile, the gearboxes were developed and strengthened.

When the 75/76/110/111 models were discontinued in August 1980, the series had set a production record (totalling over 115,000) which is unlikely ever to be surpassed.

The trucks were produced at the company's plants in Sweden, the Netherlands, Brazil and Argentina. More than 23,000 were sold on the home market, where the three-axle LS with a single driving axle was the most popular, while the twin-axle L was the model most frequently sold abroad. The three-axle LT with a double-drive bogie was rare in Sweden; in twenty-two years, a mere 526 of the 15,000 or so produced were bought by Swedish customers.

Production of the L111 totalled 30,510. The model pictured above was delivered in 1977 to a customer in Belgium, where it is still in service after an impressive 1 million kilometres on the road.

Scania LS140
1972–1976

A bonneted workhorse which became popular among timber hauliers

DEVELOPING AN IMPRESSIVE 350 HP, the new 14-litre V8 Scania engine (which had achieved great popularity since its introduction in 1969) was installed initially only in forward-control models. However, there was still a demand for bonneted trucks and, although most of its competitors had abandoned this traditional configuration, Scania decided to build a bonneted version using the new engine. As a result, the bonneted L140 and LS140 entered production in February 1972, two and a half years after their forward-control counterparts.

Since timber hauliers traditionally preferred bonneted trucks (having an engine in front on a narrow, icy forest road gave a sense of security), the new L models became popular in this particular application. However, they were also widely used for construction site and heavy-haulage work—and even as tow trucks.

(continued)

A true workhorse, Raimo Koponen's Scania LS140 was typical of the many similar forest trucks delivered to Finland in the 1970s. Operating in difficult conditions, it served its owner well, covering long distances without major technical faults. It was, at one and the same time, both a common and typically Finnish sight.

Then—as now—hauling timber in Finland was extremely tough work. With loads upwards of 70 tonnes (compared with the legal limit of 40), power was needed to get the job done. Raimo's truck covered 650,000 kilometres on rough forest roads before it was retired in 1983.

Scania LS140
(continued)

The impression of power and strength was reinforced by the broad, sloping bonnet, which was integral with the front wings and (for the first time) was made of glass fibre-reinforced plastic. The complete bonnet/wing unit tilted forward to provide access to the engine and front axle for service and repair work.

Based on the unit used in the forward-control version, the cab offered a high standard of interior comfort and space—features which had hitherto been rare in bonneted models. As a result, the L140 series became something of a favourite among drivers who preferred this type.

The L140 was equipped with a 7-tonne front axle, giving a GVW of 23 tonnes, or 500 kg more than the forward-control variants. In 1973, the gross weight was increased to 24 tonnes by the introduction of a 17-tonne bogie, to cope more efficiently with the high loads encountered particularly in forestry duties.

In 1975, Scania introduced a tandem-drive version of the L140 (the LT145 described on the following page) for the toughest of applications.

The increasingly popular practice of adorning trucks with decorative paintwork, interior fittings and chrome trim made the L140 highly prized. In technical terms, the series was little different from its forward-control LB140 counterparts (see page 104).

The bonnet and wings tilted forward as a balanced unit, providing access to the engine and front axle for service and repair work.

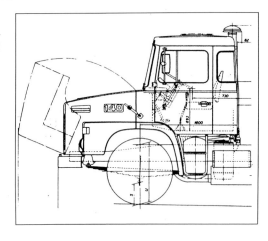

From the outset, it was equipped with the new ten-speed, GR 860 synchromesh gearbox, normally with a hypoid, single-reduction final drive. For the heaviest applications, however, this could be replaced by a two-stage rear axle/hub reduction configuration.

The L140 Series was produced from 1972 to 1976.

The fuel tank was protected by steel beams to guard against tree stumps and rocks on the atrocious forest roads, while the suspension was reinforced by an extra spring. The frame was also strengthened to cope with the stresses imposed by the rear-mounted crane with which the truck was equipped. Loading was a one-man job.

SPECIFICATIONS	
Chassis	Type LS140
Wheelbase	5.00 m
Gross weight	24,000 kg
Engine	Type DS14 (D14), V8, direct-injection, supercharged diesel
Output	350 (275) hp
Bore	127 mm
Stroke	140 mm
Swept volume	14.2 litre
No. built	1,653

WHEN CONTRACTORS SCHAKTCENTRALEN OF Karlstad took delivery of their LT145 in December 1975, there was plenty of work for heavy tractors. Many different construction projects were under way, and means of ensuring that excavators and other heavy machinery were delivered safely to site were required. Transport applications of this nature (for which the truck was purpose-built) were often carried out on poor surfaces and under atrocious conditions.

To cope with heavy loads, the truck was equipped with heavy-duty axles and frame. The all-synchromesh gearbox was a ten-speed unit consisting of a five-speed main box and a two-speed range-type planetary gearbox. Combined with the rear-axle hub reduction, this made the vehicle enormously powerful—a necessary attribute for handling a maximum gross weight of up to 30 tonnes.

The machine—usually an excavator—was loaded on a low-bed semi-trailer of the type in which the platform is below the level of the fifth-wheel coupling and rear axles. "Both myself and the truck worked hard in those days", recalls Åke 'Johan' Olofsson, who

Scania LT145
1975–1976

An extremely spacious and comfortably-equipped tractor for hauling the heaviest rigs

SPECIFICATIONS	
Chassis	Type LT145
Wheelbase	3.80 m
Gross weight	30,000 kg
Engine	Type DS14 V8
Output	350 hp
Swept volume	14.2 litre
No. built	114

drove the LT145 about 350,000 kilometres until 1981. "Most of the time, I had to drive on unsurfaced roads and on bad surfaces, but she always pulled well."

The vehicle was used mostly in and around Värmland province, always with the same semi-trailer. One major construction project which it served was the Kronoparken housing scheme in Karlstad, where the above picture was taken.

The cab on this heavy tractor featured the same driver's station as the forward-control 80 Series models. In other words, the driver enjoyed a standard of comfort, equipment and space which was vastly superior to that found in most bonneted trucks. As an example, a sunroof was standard equipment on LT145s built in Södertälje.

The Scania LT145 was designed for the heaviest applications and some of the rigs which it pulled were highly spectacular. One such combination measured up to an awesome 70 metres in length. This particular trailer, which was used in Gothenburg in the late 1970s, was equipped with eight axles, each with eight wheels, and boasted a maximum loading capacity of 200 tonnes!

'SOMETHING EXTRA SPECIAL' WAS the verdict on the engine when the CR145 appeared in 1971. Installed transversely at the rear of the bus, the engine was the normally aspirated version of the turbo referred to as the most powerful truck diesel in Europe – Scania's first 14.2-litre V8. The 260-hp rating was a little out of the ordinary in bus circles!

However, the characteristics of the engine were what set it apart. Thanks to its high swept volume and high torque, it never needed to be over-extended, performing powerfully and smoothly over the entire speed range without requiring over-frequent gear changes (a fortunate attribute since the long linkage between the gear lever and gearbox was sloppy, to say the least).

In reality, the large V8 represented an interim measure during the late 1960s, a time when Scania was attempting to develop new, competitive long-distance buses and tourist coaches to replace its front-engined models, which were now almost impossible to sell.

The required rating was approximately 250 hp – about that developed by the turbocharged version of the 11-litre engine. However, this unit was actually too long and

Scania
CR145
1971

———

A special engine

The front of the bus was an impressive sight as it hove into view in the rear-view mirror of a car – not an unusual occurrence given the speed and power of the model.

had to be inclined considerably to make it fit.

And so, the BR145 and the integrally-built CR145 were born. The V8 was a compact, if somewhat heavy, unit with more than adequate power. Less powerful versions, designated BR85 and CR85 and equipped with an inclined, 8-litre engine, were also available.

Consisting of separate front and rear sections attached to a monocoque body of conventional design, the chassis was a new concept to Scania-Bussar and, since Scania was the only manufacturer using this principle, a great deal of 'missionary' work and training was required before other coachbuilders mastered the technique. Although hardly an original design, Scania-Bussar's own body was functional and spacious and, with the perfection of the production technique in its own plant, production of the vehicle was successfully rationalised.

The model enabled Scania to maintain its position in the interurban and tourist-coach segment of the market, achieving satisfactory sales at home and in other Scandinavian countries. However, it became obsolescent when production of the normally aspirated V8 engine was discontinued in 1978.

SPECIFICATIONS	
Chassis	Type CR145
Wheelbase	6.50 m
Gross weight	15,500 kg
Engine	Type D14
Output	260 hp
Swept volume	14.2 litre
Coachbuilder	Scania-Bussar
No. of passengers	51 seated
No. built	
BR/CR85	840
BR/CR145	894

Scania LB81
1975–1981

An easy-to-drive suburban truck with an automatic gearbox option

IN THE LATE 1970s, the Scania range of trucks was constructed around seven basic models. However, it is said that all of the possible combinations would have produced about 10,000 different variants – a somewhat odd statistic which serves to emphasise the fact that it was possible to custom-design an individual vehicle especially to suit a particular application.

The LB81 was the smallest forward-control truck in the new 'Program Scania' range introduced between 1974 and 1976. In all essential respects, the model was the same as the LB80, which it superseded.

However, eagle-eyed observers could distinguish between the models without knowing the designations, since this was the year when the new, compact Scania logo appeared below the windscreen.

The LB81 was equipped with a somewhat smaller version of the forward-tilting cab introduced on the LB110 in 1968. The interior of the new unit was modified in several respects, including the installation of an improved driver's seat with electric heating. Combined with other new features such as a redesigned steering wheel and instrument

panel, as well as new interior appointments in general, this represented a substantial updating of the cab.

The LB81 was a truck which appeared in many guises – carrying palletised loads, animal feed, refuse, soft drinks, domestic heating oil and milk, to name but a few of the different types of cargo which it was used to transport. Its utility as a delivery truck in dense traffic and on short runs was emphasised by the fact that it was available with an automatic gearbox.

Scania-Bilar of Laxå converted a number of LB80s and LB81s into convenient refuse trucks. The overall height was reduced by 20 cm by lowering both the cab and suspension, making the work of the continuously embarking and disembarking crew much easier. Most of these models were automatics.

The truck was also used as a mobile drilling platform, fifteen of which were ordered by UNICEF to drill for water in Benin (west Africa), Sri Lanka and India. Manufactured by Atlas Copco, the drilling rigs were mounted on Scania LB81 chassis. (This was, incidentally, Scania's first direct delivery of vehicles to India).

SPECIFICATIONS	
Chassis	Type LB81
Wheelbase	3.63 m
Gross weight	16,500 kg
Engine	Type DS8 (D8)
Output	210 (167) hp
Swept volume	7,8 litre
No. built	12,749

Paddington Victoria
Vauxhall Peckham
New Cross Lewisham

PADDINGT

KJD 201P

Scania BR111 DH
1973–1978

Joint venture

IT WAS A BUS WHICH aroused strong emotions. How could a small Swedish company have the impertinence to believe that it could penetrate the British double-decker market, which Leyland held in an iron grip? However, this is exactly what Scania attempted to do at the beginning of the 1970s.

The process began in 1969 when Scania-Bussar undertook a joint venture with British bodybuilders, Metro-Cammel Weymann Ltd. Designers from MCW visited Katrineholm to study monocoque-body construction and prototypes were tested on the Scania vibration test track. The first eighteen vehicles (single-deckers), with a body by MCW and mechanical equipment by Scania, (BR110) were delivered in March 1971. The body was of the monocoque type exactly as in the Scania CR110, while the chassis component layout was the same.

The interest which the Metro-Scania buses attracted was due to the many features which made them more modern than their British counterparts. These included the monocoque body with its low floor, the powerful engine, the automatic gearbox and the air suspension, while the well-designed heating system was a further bonus.

(continued)

A Swedish double-decker in British city traffic. Although the bus was not particularly 'Swedish', the method of construction and the Scania chassis made it special in several respects. The centre aisle was unusually low thanks to the special design of the front and rear axles, while the air suspension offered a standard of riding comfort above the ordinary.

Scania BR111 DH
(continued)

The power steering was far too light in the opinion of London Transport management, who requested that it be made heavier in case drivers should demand that the rest of the fleet should be just as easy to drive!

The joint venture received considerable attention in the British press, which reported – among other things – that women (!) had been seen driving Scania city buses in Sweden. Although the standard of riding comfort attracted generally favourable comment, the fact that the chassis were being imported at a time when the British bus industry was facing one of its recurrent crises created bad blood. The argument that only a minor proportion of the vehicles' value was of Swedish origin cut little ice. The buses were imports, it was maintained, and represented "a knife in the back of British Leyland!"

In time, however, the storm abated and several orders followed. So satisfactory were the vehicles in service that Scania and MCW decided jointly to build a double-decker. Designated the BR111 DH, the chassis was based largely on ordinary BR111 components. The model was christened the 'Metropolitan' by MCW. To create a low central aisle running the full length of the bus, the front axle height was lowered and the rear axle designed with an offset banjo casing.

On this occasion also, a prototype underwent trials (including a series of vibration tests) at Södertälje before MCW received approval for series production. However, city traffic conditions in Britain exceeded the vibration-test stress levels, making it necessary to strengthen the front axle and rear suspension, and to replace the Scania HR501 automatic gearbox with the new GAV764

Power steering made the BR111 easy to handle in city traffic — too easy in the opinion of some! In addition, air suspension offered a ride out of the ordinary.

unit to prolong the life of the transmission. In addition, the British-built bodies displayed a tendency to rust.

Combined with massive 'Buy British' campaigns, these problems led to the demise of the joint venture in 1978, hastened by the fact that the companies were in disagreement over the correct market segment for the model. Whereas Scania was disposed to spread the sales among smaller operators throughout Britain, MCW's philosophy was to concentrate on the larger urban transport utilities. As a result, MCW developed its own double-decker, while Scania continued to export about 100 double-decker chassis annually to Britain during most of the 1980s.

In all, 133 BR111 single-decker chassis and 663 BR111 DH double-decker versions (including 164 for London Transport) were supplied to MCW between 1971 and 1978, while a number of others were exported to markets including Hong Kong.

The wide double doors at the front were unusual for the British market, while the aisle level was particularly low, thanks to the special design of the front and rear axles.

SPECIFICATIONS

Chassis	Type BR111 DH
Wheelbase	5.1 m
Gross weight	16,700 kg
Engine	Type D11, 6-cylinder, direct-injection diesel
Output	203 hp
Swept volume	11.0 litre
Bodybuilder	Metro-Cammell Weymann Ltd.
No. of passengers	87 (72 seated)
No. built	663

DURING THE 1970s, the density of traffic in Sweden's major urban centres increased steadily, while length limitations and other restrictions were imposed on trucks in these areas. Meanwhile, social development was imposing ever-greater demands on the fast, reliable distribution of goods.

These conditions prompted the need for a compact truck with a high payload. Oil companies and other distributors required a model capable of carrying heavy loads without the need for a trailer, enabling them to maximise the tonnage carried on every run and to minimise their operating costs.

The answer was the LBFS111, Scania's first four-axle model.

A truck with two rear axles and twin steered front axles offers many advantages in urban traffic. The extra rear axle enables the payload to be increased without increasing the length of the vehicle.

With an overall length of 10.5 metres, the LBFS111 was capable of carrying 20 m³ of fuel oil as a tanker, or 14.5 tonnes of goods as a general cargo or container truck. It provided exactly what distributors had been wait-

Scania LBFS111 1978–1980

Specially-built to carry high payloads in built-up areas

ing for – high load capacity without the need for a trailer.

Excellent stability and handling were among the other advantages of this special-purpose vehicle. The rear overhang was short, improving traffic safety for other road users in urban areas.

In the opinion of drivers, the fact that the turning radius was about a metre greater than in a conventional three-axle truck did not have a significant effect on the handling characteristics.

The LBFS111 was one of Scania's most unusual trucks. Only 39 examples were produced , 22 of them for export.

SPECIFICATIONS	
Chassis	Type LBFS111
Wheelbase	5.90 m
Gross weight	28,500 kg
Engine	Type DS11, 6-cylinder, direct-injection, supercharged diesel
Output	280 hp, 296 hp and 305 hp
Bore	127 m
Stroke	145 m
Swept volume	11,0 litre
Payload	Approx. 18,000 kg
No. built	39

IN THE TRUCK SECTOR, development trends in the 1970s were characterized by three goals—higher power, lower fuel consumption and reduced exhaust emissions. Economy became the primary concern as the transport industry faced the fact that oil resources were not inexhaustible. Environmental problems came to the fore as fuel prices rose, while the demand for transport efficiency and quality increased steadily. Concepts such as logistics, just-in-time, energy efficiency and systemised transport became the jargon in the industry.

Scania introduced the 111 Series to succeed the 110 in 1974. An increase in output, lower fuel consumption and reduced emission levels were among the features offered by the 11-litre engines. The V8 engines introduced in 1976 with the unveiling of the 141 and 146 models offered the same features. The DS14 was now rated at 375 hp—an increase of 25 hp—again making Scania the leader in terms of engine power in the heavy standard-truck sector, while the tandem-driven LT146 (now with a 30-tonne train weight) was even better suited to the heaviest applications.

In technological terms, chassis development kept pace with the demand for systemised transport and interchangeable load carriers. By 1977, Scania was offering pneumatic rear suspension as an alternative to the conventional leaf-spring type.

Italy was one of the markets to which Scania gained entry with the aid of the 141. Placing his faith in the make as EEC import restrictions were eased, Armando Rangoni, a Fiat dealer from Trento in north-eastern Italy, founded Italscandia in 1974. Resigning his Fiat agency, Rangoni secured the sole import rights for Scania in Italy, signalling the start of a fruitful relationship.

Scania LB141 1976–1981

With its raw power, the 375-hp V8 LB141 opened the Italian market to Scania trucks

Right: This 1977 LB141 was one of the first delivered to Italy, where it is still in service with foodstuffs hauliers Lapiana of Trento in the north-east of the country. Originally used on international routes, the 14-year-old truck is now kept for shorter domestic runs.

Left: The LB141 pictured here was bought by Containers Transport, a small Sicilian company, in 1977. After covering a million kilometres, carrying grain to Sardinia and returning with loads of granite blocks, it was retired and renovated by Italscandia, the Scania importer in Italy. Today, the truck is part of Scania's collection of veteran models.

The 20,000th Scania truck was delivered to Italy in 1990. In the Italian market, Scania is presently the second largest marque in the heavy-truck sector, hard on the heels of Iveco, the domestic maker. The trucks are serviced by thirty authorised dealers and about 115 independent workshops. Customer loyalty among Scania owners is high. Ninety percent are repeat buyers—testimony to the high standard of service and personal contact maintained by Italscandia with its customers.

Lapiana of Trento is just one customer from those early days when Armando Rangoni was building up Italscandia. Now international hauliers, the company was founded in 1971 to transport foodstuffs.

Operating a fleet of fifty-two Scanias, Lapiana carries a considerable proportion of the foodstuffs exported from Italy to northern Europe. Italy is highly dependent on road haulage, which accounts for 150 million tonnes annually or 85% of total freight traffic.

SPECIFICATIONS	
Chassis	Type LB141
Wheelbase	3.40 m
Gross weights	GVW 18,000 kg; GCW 43,200 kg
Engine	Type DS14, V8, direct-injection, turbocharged diesel
Output	375 hp
Bore	127 mm
Stroke	140 mm
Swept volume	14.2 litre
No. built	9,227

1980–1990

During the decade, Scania climbed to fourth position among the world's heavy-truck manufacturers. Invoiced sales increased from SKr8.2 billion to SKr24 billion, and profits from SKr1.4 billion to a peak of SKr3.8 billion. Exports exceeded 90%. Bus production reached a record of 3,800 deliveries in 1989. A total of over 30,000 vehicles was produced for the first time in 1987 and, two years later, this figure was exceeded by truck exports alone. The manufacture of engines and gearboxes for Saab cars was discontinued with the merger between GM and Saab. In 1988, sales of VW vehicles totalled 46,240, the highest level since 1965.

In 1980, SCANIA INTRODUCED the first models in a completely new truck series with designations ending in '2', when the T82, T112 and T142 were unveiled. The major new features of the series were its advanced level of component standardisation and the high level of comfort which it offered in bonneted models.

Using a limited number of engines, gearboxes, axles, final drives, frames and cabs, the range could be varied to suit the most

**Scania
T112 H 4×2
1980–**

———

*Introducing
standard-
component
Scania trucks*

diverse transport applications. Three chassis classes—M (medium-duty), H (heavy-duty) and E (extra heavy-duty)—with gross weights ranging from 16 to 36 tonnes, were available. Other innovations included new generations of engines with higher output and torque ratings, offering lower fuel consumption and cleaner exhaust emissions.

In 1981, the series was augmented by the forward-control 82, 112 and 142 models, all incorporating the basic elements of the Ital-

diesels made its appearance. The first of these was an 8-litre version, which was followed a year later by charge-cooled versions of both the 11-litre and 14-litre units. The technique of cooling the charge air delivered by the compressor in a turbocharged engine enabled higher output to be developed without impairing fuel consumption or emission levels.

The T112 is powered by a six-cylinder, in-line, charge-cooled, 333-hp engine driving a ten-speed range gearbox. The model is often used as a tractor to haul semi-trailers in heavy, medium-haul applications in which the extremely high power of the V8 is not required.

Germany is one of Scania's most important European export markets. With imports running at approximately 1,600 trucks per annum, about 11,000 German-registered Scanias are in service at present, keeping the nation on the move.

Germans love their beer, and no less than 35,000,000 litres are distributed daily throughout the country in the large tankers and smaller delivery trucks which have long since replaced the horse.

The firm of Alt-Bier-Brauerei was founded in the city of Düsseldorf in 1873. Originally a local brewery using horse-drawn drays to supply distribution outlets with its products, the company now supplies the entire Ruhr with its popular Frankenheim Alt beer.

One of the modern workhorses which is still used to ensure that supplies of Frankenheim Alt reach their destinations is a Scania T112 and trailer, a lavishly decorated rig which carries 23,000 litres of the amber liquid.

ian-designed cabs with their modern standards of comfort. In the different versions, the basic cab was finished simply by adding back panels, sides, doors and bonnets of different heights, the designations G, P and R being used to denote the cab sizes. With the GPRT range, Scania had progressed further towards rational component standardisation than any of its competitors.

The 2 Series witnessed the advent of charge-air cooling as the 'third generation' of

This German T112 is used to distribute beer from Alt-Bier-Brauerei in Düsseldorf to thousands of customers in the Ruhr. With a capacity of 23,000 litres, the rig covers about 60,000 km annually.

SPECIFICATIONS	
Chassis	Type T112 H 4x2
Wheelbase	4.60 m
Gross weight	16,000 kg (trailer 22,000 kg)
Engine	Type DSC11 (DN11 or DS11)
	6-cylinder, direct-injection, turbo-charged diesel with charge cooling
Output	333 (203, 280 or 305) hp
Bore	127 mm
Stroke	145 mm
Swept volume	11.0 litre
No. built	33,100 (to 1990 incl.)

Scania K buses 1982-

The company's most successful bus chassis in all categories

Scania almost lost its grip on the interurban and tourist coach market before the BR85 and BR145 rescued the situation in 1971 (see page 118). With front-engined chassis no longer marketable in Europe, the BR/CR145 kept the flag flying until 1978, when the normally-aspirated version of the V8 engine was discontinued, leaving Scania-Bussar without either an engine or a bus in this particular segment.

Its replacement, the BR116 (chassis only), provided an indication of what the market required. Developing 305 hp, the longitudinally mounted, 11-litre, turbocharged, six-cylinder unit was one of the most powerful available, while the light, robust chassis offered attractive driving characteristics.

Scania-Bussar incorporated these features in the new range, introduced in 1982. The BR116 was developed into the K112 (or the K82 with an 8-litre engine). Component standardisation between trucks and buses had been pursued as far as possible with the aim of creating a 'world' model – one which could be sold, alongside the company's trucks, even in less-developed markets.

Success followed quickly. The model immediately proved a best-seller and was to become the highest-selling Scania bus chassis of all time.

In 1984, the K82 was succeeded by the K92, which was powered by Scania's new 9-litre engine. At this time, the K112 also became available with the option of a charge air-cooled, 11-litre unit. Developing 333 hp, this made the model a long-distance cruiser.

A new generation of chassis, the 3 Series, appeared in 1988. The K92 and K112 now became the K93 and K113 respectively (developing outputs of up to 363 hp), while the charge air-cooled, low-emission DSC11 was also added to the range.

The power developed by a bus is dictated not by the 'joy of speed', but by practical considerations. It is no longer accepted that long-distance buses lose speed on hills or hinder other traffic. Furthermore, given adequate power, the passenger's journey will be restful despite a high average speed.

Otherwise, the strength of the range lies in its versatility. The chassis is suitable not only for interurban buses and tourist coaches, but also for urban and suburban models in markets in which a low floor is not of decisive importance. The chassis consists of a

front and a rear sub-frame which, together with the body, form a monocoque construction providing enormous baggage space between the front and rear axles. A 'frame-type' chassis is available as a simple and robust all-round solution.

The range of options also extends to chassis and drive trains. Air suspension (now the

The Bel Tour Company operates tourist services in Rio de Janeiro. This Neilson-bodied K112 T is one of its 40-strong fleet. The high-built model offers a superb view.

predominant type) has recently been enhanced with new features such as kneeling, which facilitates boarding, and ground clearance adjustment, which permits the bus to be driven comfortably onto a ferry without scraping the underside on the ramp. Individual front-wheel suspension enables the floor level to be made extremely low at the front,

Spain is one of Scania's most important bus markets. Pictured in Tenerife, this K113 is part of the Alpitours tourist coach fleet. The body was built by Irizar.

while braking systems have become even more reliable and anti-lock brakes are practically standard on modern long-distance models.

CAG (Computed-Aided Gearchanging) has made the task of the coachbuilder – as well as the driver – even simpler. This new electronic system eliminates mechanical linkages between the driver's station and the gearbox while, on certain models, the throttle linkage has been replaced by a 'drive-by-wire' system. Automatic gearboxes have also been equipped with electronic control systems.

Several other models have sprung from

The bus is unquestionably the most important means of long-distance passenger transport in Argentina. The robust chassis of the Scania K113 T is ideally suited to this type of demanding service, which sometimes involves journeys of over 5,000 kilometres.

the successful K range. Scania's first bogie-mounted bus, the K112 T, was introduced in 1984 and a bodied K bus (CK112) appeared in 1987. This was followed, in 1989, by the L113, in which the floor level at the rear was lowered by using a chassis with an inclined engine.

The K range has become renowned worldwide. Introduced into production within a short period at the company's plants in Sweden, Argentina and Brazil, the models have taken over much of the role of the front-engined bus as a simple and robust all-round chassis.

SPECIFICATIONS	
Chassis	Type K112 T
Wheelbase	6.90 m
Gross weight	22,800 kg
Engine	Type DS11, 6-cylinder, direct-injection diesel
Output	305 hp
Swept volume	11.02 litre
Bodybuilder	Nielson
No. of passengers	42 seated
No. built	K112 T/113 T: 2,424
	K82/92/93/112/113: 14,854

Scania's entry into the articulated bus market was a long time coming. Although the use of a conventional rear-engined chassis was considered out of the question (since the engine would be in the way of the articulated joint), pusher-type articulated models with the engine at the extreme rear, driving the wheels of the 'trailer', had been built in the early 1970s, particularly in West Germany.

Articulated buses became more common in Sweden—especially on longer suburban routes—after the changeover to right-hand traffic in 1967. Most were built on chassis with the engine amidships driving the intermediate axle and with steered wheels at the rear—a model which was easy to build but was difficult to manoeuvre when reversing or negotiating sharp bends, given the tendency of the rear wheels to understeer.

In late 1978, Scania-Bussar decided to develop a pusher prototype in collaboration with the German company, Schenk, who were experts in the field, and the Belgian coachbuilders, Jonckheere. The model was based on the BR112, the 'silent' city and suburban chassis, with the power unit simply relocated at the extreme rear. The driver op-

Scania CN112 A 1984–1989

An easy-to-drive pusher-type articulated bus

erated the engine by means of a newly-developed electrical system.

The risk of 'jackknifing' of the articulated joint in icy weather presented the only major problem. However, the expertise of Schenk and Jonckheere in this area proved invaluable and a design which eliminated the risk by electronic means was developed in collaboration with Scania. Combined with anti-lock brakes, the result was a safe, easy-to-drive vehicle.

As Scania's first articulated bus chassis, the N112 A entered production in 1983 (the designation having been changed the previous year) and was succeeded a year later by the integrally-built CN112 A.

SPECIFICATIONS	
Chassis	Type CN112 A
Wheelbase	6.05 + 5.03 m
Overall length	18 m
Gross weight	27,500 kg
Engine	Type DS11
Output	253 hp
Swept volume	11.0 litre
Bodybuilder	Scania-Bussar
No. of passengers	Approx. 120 (74 seated)
No. built	100 (149)

HEADED BY THE FLAGSHIP R143, the Scania 3 Series was introduced in autumn 1987. After an interval of some years, European truckmakers were again jostling for position in the ratings league and model after model was appearing in the 'almost 500-hp' class.

Higher outputs were required not only to cope with the heaviest duties, such as forestry and contracting applications involving high payloads, but also to comply with ever-tougher scheduling requirements and constantly high average speeds in long-haul traffic.

With a proud tradition of engine development to uphold, Scania was in the forefront of events. The company was also the first European manufacturer to introduce a mass-produced diesel with electronic fuel injection (known as Electronic Diesel Control, or EDC). As the successor to the turbo/charge-cooled diesels, the R143 now heralded the electronic age, introducing technology already familiar from systems such as electronically controlled anti-lock brakes and automatic gearchanging.

Equipped with a turbocharger, charge-air cooler and EDC, the V8 developed 470 hp. In keeping with Scania's low-revs philosophy, maximum power was developed at only 1,900 r/min, although the engine speed could be increased to 2,100 r/min to skip a gear or to avoid changing.

The exterior concealed many new engine refinements which not only yielded higher output, but also ensured low fuel consumption and longer life, while complying with European emission standards by a margin of 20%. Provision for adding features such as cruise control and a smoke limiter were included 'as a bonus'. Buyers of the R143 had a choice of three V8 engines, developing 400, 450 and 470 hp respectively.

A new ten-speed gearbox, designed for the prevailing torques of almost 2,000 Nm, was also introduced to handle the high engine outputs. A range-type synchromesh unit which could also be equipped with computer-aided gearchanging (CAG), the new gearbox afforded easier shifting, shorter changing movements and smaller intervals between the highest gears.

However, the cab design was the most striking new feature of the series. The elegant interior, with the instrument panel curved around the driver's position, was con-

Scania R143 ML 4×2 1988–

Europe's first mass-produced truck with electronic fuel injection (EDC). A new long-haul cab with air suspension has earned the model several distinctions.

This R143 is one of eighteen Scanias used by the French family haulage firm of Lebrun to transport wine. Each day, the truck hauls a trailer loaded with 12,000 bottles of vintage wines from Champagne. The truck is, appropriately, equipped with air suspension to protect the valuable cargo.

sidered by many observers to be the most attractive in any make of truck. The driver was, literally, at the centre of things, surrounded by modular instruments positioned according to their frequency of use.

Extremely comfortable seating and excellent vision, ergonomically positioned controls, a quietly lavish interior, an elevated roof in the long-haul cab (which also boasted

level-controlled air suspension), standing room, generous space for changing in front of a completely stowable passenger seat, central locking and many other features were among the refinements for which the Scania 3 Series was voted European 'Truck of the Year' in 1989, and for which it received several other awards for outstanding driver comfort.

In 1990, 19,000 Scania trucks were operating on French roads. These are serviced by a steadily expanding network of about forty dealers and eighty workshops. Scania will open a 50,000-m² truck assembly plant in Anger in 1991.

SPECIFICATIONS	
Chassis	Type R143ML 4x2
Wheelbase	4.60 m
Gross weight	18,000 kg
Engine	Type DSC14 (alt. DS14 or DSC14) V8, direct-injection diesel
Output	450 (alt. 400 or 470) hp
Swept volume	14.2 litre
No. built	737 (to 1990 incl.)

Scania
G93 ML 4×2
1988–

A modern delivery truck with three different variants of Scania's smallest engine. The low-entry G model is designed to facilitate the driver's work.

THE SCANIA G MODEL was nicknamed the 'Geisha' when the technical details of the new GPRT range were announced in 1980. Equipped with an extra-low step to make life easier for the driver, the model was designed for delivery applications in which he was required to enter and leave the cab constantly.

For the first time, the new GPRT range offered buyers the facility of specifying cabs, chassis, drive trains and suspensions to suit particular applications. Like the P82, the 'light' G82 delivery truck (GVW 16 tonnes) was designed to carry high-volume cargoes. Since this was a matter of maximising the cargo space (in other words, of locating the body or platform as close as possible to the cab), the turbo and cab rear suspension were both relocated further forward, the gear-selector mechanism modified and the air intake lowered—all with the object of clearing the frame of 'obstructions' behind the cab.

'G' was the designation assigned to the lowest cab, which was combined with the Type 82 chassis or, from 1985 on, with the Type 92. In that year, Scania also introduced a new generation of its smallest engines by increasing the swept volume of the straight-six, 8-litre unit, and equipping it with a new injection system, separate cylinder heads

(continued)

This Danish-registered truck delivers beer and soft drinks daily from the Tuborg depot in Odense to customers in the northern area of Funen Island. It is pictured here at the birth-place of Hans-Christian Andersen, the celebrated Danish writer.

Scania
G93 ML 4×2
(continued)

and other mechanical improvements to create a practically new 9-litre engine boasting low fuel consumption, low weight, high efficiency and low speed—all invaluable features in delivery applications. The new engine was available either with a turbo, or with both a turbo and charge cooler.

Four different rating classes from 211 to 282 hp were introduced successively to meet a wide range of requirements, while delivery-truck engines now progressed to the next generation—the charge-cooler age. A new 211-hp unit was introduced in the special Scania City model, a large, light delivery truck combining high payload with high power.

In 1983, Scania had become the first truckmaker to introduce its revolutionary microprocessor-controlled gearbox for delivery trucks. This was a mechanical 'automatic' gearbox designed to simplify the work of the driver, especially in delivery trucks, and also in cleaning trucks and service vehicles. Known as CAG (Computer-Aided Gearchanging), this heralded the advent of electronics in trucks, and was followed by other systems such as electronically controlled anti-lock brakes (ABS), electronic fuel injection (known as Electronic Diesel Control or EDC) and electronic braking (ELB).

The G92 was superseded by the G93 when Scania unveiled its new 3 Series in 1988. With a wheelbase of up to 5.8 metres, the

The curved instrument panel in the G93 gives the driver easy access to all of the controls without leaning forward.

new model was tailor-made for superstructures such as a box body, demountable body, or platform and crane. Special springing was installed in an extra-low-level version used as a refuse truck.

The versatility of the G93 was widened by options ranging from a five or ten-speed manual gearbox to a fully automatic four-speed transmission or the intermediate option of CAG. Naturally, pneumatic rear suspension was also available for load-handling applications and for enhanced driving comfort.

SPECIFICATIONS	
Chassis	Type G93 ML 4x2
Wheelbase	5.80 m
Gross weight	16,000 kg
Engine	Type DS9, 6-cylinder, direct-injection, turbocharged diesel
Output	210 hp
Bore	115 mm
Stroke	136 mm
Swept volume	8.5 litre
No. built	891 (to 1990 incl.)

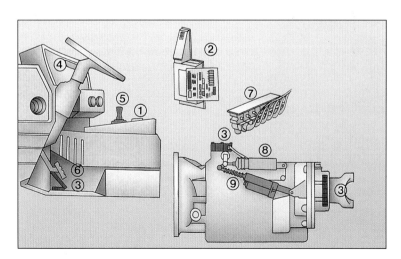

How CAG works: The driver operates the gearbox by means of a small selector lever (5) and selector switch (1) which is used to select the driving mode (automatic or manual changing, reverse or neutral). The brain of the system is a microprocessor (2) which is supplied by sensors with information describing the throttle position (3), driving speed and gear engaged. These signals are processed continuously to keep the driver informed—by means of a small display (4) on the instrument panel—of which gear should be selected at any time. The driver initiates a change by depressing the clutch pedal (6) and the microprocessor 'changes gear' with the aid of the solenoid valves (7) which control the actuating cylinders (8). Item (9) is a damping cylinder.

ALL-WHEEL DRIVE OFFERS significant advantages in difficult conditions, demonstrating its superiority when operating on loose ground, on steep, slippery slopes and in stony terrain. As an example, conditions on new construction sites are usually the worst imaginable—and the truck is usually the first vehicle on site. Consequently, it must be capable of operating efficiently and profitably without getting bogged down.

The new 3 Series includes 4x4 and 6x6 models built for rugged applications of this nature. Based on long experience of military vehicles, Scania's all-wheel-drive trucks offer a standard of mobility, running economy and payload capacity which meet the high demands of the civilian sector also.

The Scania P113 HK 6x6 is available with a choice of 310-hp, 320-hp and 363-hp engines, all six-cylinder turbocharged units. The more powerful versions are also equipped with a charge-air cooler.

The six wheels are driven through a main gearbox and a two-position transfer unit. Selecting the lower of the positions increases

Scania P113 HK 6×6 1988-

An all-wheel-drive vehicle for rugged service on poor surfaces

SPECIFICATIONS	
Chassis	Type P113 HK 6x6
Wheelbase	4.25 m
Gross weight	28,000 kg
Engine	Type DS11 (DSC11)
Output	310, 320 or 363 hp
Swept volume	11.0 litre
No. built	242 (to 1990 incl.)

the tractive effort in each of the ten main gearbox speeds by 50%, while each axle is equipped with a differential lock to improve mobility even further.

The all-wheel-drive trucks are fitted with the same practical and comfortable cab as other Scania 3-Series models. The air filter—which efficiently purifies all air entering the cab—is a feature particularly appreciated by drivers, especially on dusty sites.

The Norwegian army has ordered over 1,500 Scania cross-country trucks—all specials based on all-wheel-drive 3-Series chassis. Delivery is scheduled for completion in 1995. In addition to meeting normal requirements, the trucks are designed to negotiate water up to 80 cm deep.

Fifty-two of the vehicles are of the Scania P113 HK 6x6 type pictured above. These will be equipped with towing cranes and winches manufactured by Hägglunds-Moelv in Norway.

Scania
Turbocompound
1991

—

An even more efficient diesel engine

SCANIA WILL BECOME THE first manufacturer in the world to undertake series production of a turbocompound truck engine when it launches its new unit in 1991 (the company's centenary year)—an event which will herald a new era in more than half a century of diesel engine development.

In the 1930s, the efficiency of the diesel engine was about 30%. In other words, less than one-third of the energy which it con-

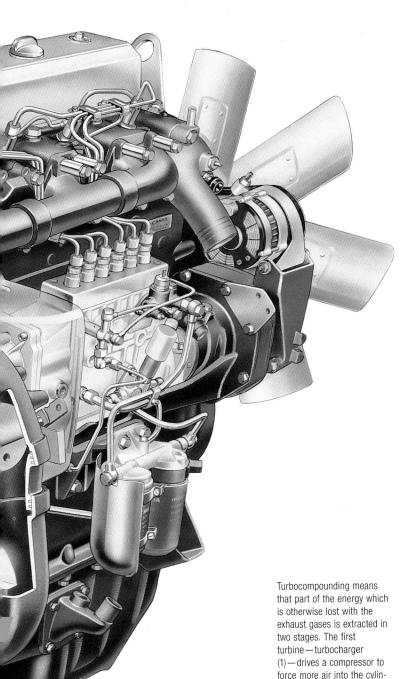

The Scania DTC11 (as the new unit is known) has an efficiency of 46% compared with the 44% offered by the most efficient of today's charge-cooled diesels. Thus, the efficiency of the diesel is approaching 50% while modern petrol engines return only 30 to 35%.

The turbocompound unit is based on Scania's classic 11-litre six, which is still the leader in its field. Features include turbocharging, charge-cooling, electronic fuel injection (EDC) and an exhaust-driven power turbine. Turbocompounding (TC) means that the residual energy of the exhaust gases is utilised at a later stage, downstream of the turbocharger. The power developed by the power turbine is returned to the flywheel, increasing engine output and efficiency alike. Power and torque are about 5% higher at 400 hp and 1,750 Nm compared with an equivalent charge-cooled engine with EDC. The improvement in efficiency is mirrored by the specific fuel consumption of 186 g/kWh, a saving of 6 g/kWh. Like all Scania engines introduced in 1991, the turbocompound engine complies with the forthcoming 1993 European emission control standards.

The superb flexibility or 'driveability' of the turbocompound engine is obvious on the road. In terms of performance, it matches far bulkier and heavier engines of higher capacity.

Turbocompounding means that part of the energy which is otherwise lost with the exhaust gases is extracted in two stages. The first turbine — turbocharger (1) — drives a compressor to force more air into the cylinders, while the second — power turbine (2) — supplies additional power to the flywheel (4) through an hydraulic coupling and gear train (3).

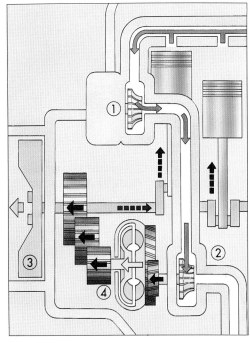

sumed was converted into useful work. Although a seemingly modest figure, this was far superior to that offered by contemporary petrol engines, and was better than that of the diesel's forerunner, the Hesselman engine.

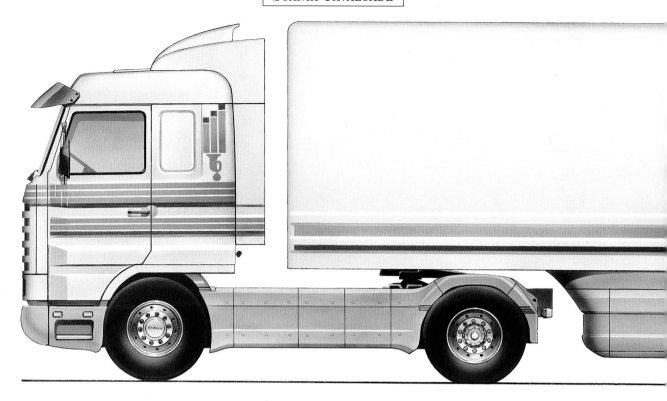

Scania's position at the leading edge of automotive technology is maintained by the Streamline cab, in which an exceptionally aerodynamic shape of the type normally seen only on experimental vehicles at motor shows has been translated into reality in a unit that is custom-designed for series production.

Scania Streamline 1991

Total vehicle concept produces results

The aerodynamic drag coefficient (Cd) has been lowered to almost 0.5—12 to 15% less than basic models—reducing long-haul fuel consumption by 2–3 litres per 100 km, or 4–5%. Based on an annual mileage of 120,000 kilometres, this yields a saving of between 2,400 and 3,600 litres of diesel fuel.

An improvement in fuel economy of this order is a significant advance. The cumulative effects of reduced drag and higher engine efficiency achieved in the ten years since the introduction of the GPRT range represent an average fuel saving of 12%.

Transport capacities have also increased during this period. Payloads have risen as a result of lower chassis weights and higher legal gross weights, while engines have become more powerful, enabling higher average speeds to be attained. In addition, rising fuel costs highlight the savings to be gained from operating more sophisticated equipment to reduce fuel consumption.

Sophistication is the hallmark of the Streamline cab; not a single detail has been left to chance.

The basic structure of the cab is identical to that of the Scania R range. While the upper section of the unit remains unchanged, the front (including the bumper) is completely new, featuring smoothly rounded contours

with corner radii of 270 mm, and flush-mounted headlamps and indicators. The doors are fitted with 'spats' extending downward to cover the top two steps, giving the side of the cab smooth, even lines while keeping the steps clean.

Two air scoops, which direct a flow of air along the sides of the cab through a series of slits, are located close to the headlamps. Combined with the wedge shape of the door extensions, this helps to prevent wheel spray from spattering the doors and windows.

Since every gap along the sides of a vehicle interferes with air flow, the cab and body should ideally be integral to ensure unimpeded air flow.

The fact that most modern vehicles run on low-profile tyres has enabled the size of the wheel arch openings to be minimised. Side skirts are available to 'dress' the chassis between the front and rear wheels. These are designed especially to minimise turbulence along the sides of articulated vehicles. As before, the gap between the cab and the body is effectively bridged by Scania's air deflector kit, which is designed to perform this function without creating unwanted turbulence.

However, 'gimmicks' such as skirts and fairings cannot be allowed to interfere with the maintenance of a working vehicle. Thus,

An optimised tractor/semi-trailer rig with a Streamline cab, air deflectors and side skirts boasts a drag coefficient of 0.5.

the skirts on the Streamline—while keeping the chassis clean and eliminating some noise—are easy to remove. The front grille opens high for daily checks and two foldaway steps are built into the front bumper to facilitate cleaning of the windscreen. The cab tilt pump is mounted inside the bumper on the near side of the truck, away from traffic.

This combination of features maximises the aerodynamic properties of the Scania Streamline—an area in which the total vehicle concept is that most likely to produce truly effective results.

The smoke trails in the wind tunnel are merciless in revealing turbulence. In all, development of the Streamline took more than 40,000 hours over a four-year period.

Index

Notes

Product names
VABIS (for Vagnfabriks-Aktiebolaget i Södertelge) and Scania (for Maskinfabriksaktiebolaget Scania i Malmö) were used until the companies merged in 1911. Scania-Vabis was used from then until the introduction of the Program Scania range in 1968, when the present name of Scania was adopted.
Details in specification boxes

Chassis: Information in () indicates supplementary type designation.
Wheelbase: Distance between first front axle and first drive axle. In the case of three-axle vehicles, the distance between the bogie axles is also stated e.g. 3.55 + 1.48 m. Other wheelbases may also be specified.
Gross weight: In the case of trucks, normally the gross weight officially registered. In the case of buses built from 1945 on, the maximum

permissible total weight specified by the manufacturer. As used only for buses built prior to 1945, the term denotes the kerb weight plus the weight of the permissible number of passengers, quantity of baggage and goods.
Engine: The company's internal designation is given in () in the case of vehicles built from 1914 to 1927. Alternative engine type designations are given in () for vehicles built after 1944.

Output: Rated outputs of alternative engines are given in (). Non-Swedish rating standards were used for certain series built for export markets from 1974 to 1980. In such cases, the output specified is that pertaining to the country of registration of the vehicle featured in the article.
Swept volume: Synonymous with cubic capacity and displacement, this term is used throughout for the sake of uniformity. 'Cubic capacity' was

used internally by the company until the more modern term 'swept volume' was adopted with the introduction of the 81, 86, 111, 141 and 146 series.
No. built: The number produced with the same type designation as the featured vehicle. In some cases, the total number of vehicles built with a similar chassis is given in ().